NINE HABITS OF
TRULY TRANSFORMED PEOPLE

The Power to Become an Effective Christian

DAVID R. HOPKINS, Ed. D.

Foreword by Vinson Synan, Ph. D.

Printed by
LifeSprings Resources
Franklin Springs, Georgia

ENDORSEMENTS

Dr. David Hopkins has written a challenging book on the habits of a transformed life. The fruit of the Spirit is presented as the natural outgrowth of a believer's relationship with Christ. This book will challenge and inspire the reader to a higher standard of discipleship than is prevalent in our culture today. Dr. Hopkins has successfully woven many practical stories and anecdotes from his own life and those of his friends throughout the book.

Nine Habits of Truly Transformed People *is an excellent personal guide to a more Christlike life. It can also serve as an effective study course for small groups seeking to develop true discipleship.*

Presiding Bishop James D. Leggett, General Superintendent
International Pentecostal Holiness Church

The Spirit-filled life must reveal the fruit of the Spirit. David Hopkins has not only written about the fruit but has consistently demonstrated the effectiveness of the fruit of the Spirit in his own life and ministry. In a brief but powerful manner, this book takes the reader deeper in the joy and fruitfulness of a godly life!

Dr. A. D. Beacham, Jr., Executive Director of World Missions
International Pentecostal Holiness Church

We live in a noisy world that has become drunk on success, instant gratification, and selfishness. That's why it is so refreshing to read David Hopkins' simple but powerful message about the fruit of the Holy Spirit. We desperately need the nine qualities that are explained in Nine Habits of Truly Transformed People—*in our churches, in the workplace, at school, at home, and in the halls of government. I know that David Hopkins has walked with God for many years, and he is not just writing about these concepts. He lives them.*

J. Lee Grady, Editor
Charisma magazine

Everyone, seemingly, is offering steps or habits to make one successful. Now Dr. David Hopkins zeroes in precisely on Jesus' standard of success and fulfillment in life—the fruit of the Spirit or Christlikeness. Nine Habits of Truly Transformed People *provides clear definitions and explanations of each fruit of the Holy Spirit so true character transformation can be realized by all Christians.*

Dr. Garnet E. Pike, Dean of the Graduate School
Southwestern Christian University

Dr. David Hopkins has written a timely and needed book when more interest seems to be in the gifts of the Spirit, which reflect the benevolence of the Giver, than the fruit of the Spirit, which tests the maturity of the believer. Who better to write a book like this than one who has demonstrated the power of God to produce the fruit through the oftentimes painful process of spiritual maturation?

Rev. Barbara Tengan, Senior Pastor
Wailuku Door of Faith Church, Maui, Hawaii

For 25 years I have witnessed the life of the author of Nine Habits of Truly Transformed People. *The basic test of an author's work is his knowledge of his subject. David Hopkins writes from experience and from his heart the message needed by all of us who call ourselves children of the King. The language is clear, the message is relevant, and the challenge is poignant. One may not read this book and settle back into mediocrity in his Christian walk without a clear probe of the Holy Spirit impelling him to shine in the darkening world. Transformed people must be different, and the author reveals that difference in comparisons, contrasts, analogies, examples, and scriptural truth.*

Dr. G. Earl Beatty, Executive Vice President
Emmanuel College

NINE HABITS OF
TRULY TRANSFORMED PEOPLE

TABLE OF CONTENTS

FOREWORD

I have known David Hopkins since he enrolled as a freshman at Emmanuel College in Franklin Springs, Georgia, in 1959. I remember him as a very bright student who clearly showed that he had gifts of scholarship and leadership. He was a very active student who engaged in many activities on campus. He was best known for singing in a gospel quartet that traveled a great deal promoting the College. His wife, Claudia, served as my faculty secretary for a year. She was a very engaging and efficient worker.

I also knew David as coming from a very prominent family in the Church. The Hopkins family provided leading pastors in Virginia, North Carolina, and Georgia. His father, Paul Hopkins, impressed me greatly by earning his bachelor's degree at the University of Memphis at 40 years of age! David Hopkins sprang from good and solid roots. I also had the privilege of serving on the faculty at Emmanuel College with David. He was a fine English teacher and was soon recognized as a future leader of the College. His dissertation for the Doctor of Education degree at the University of Georgia (1974) was a comparative history of the six voluntary regional accrediting associations in America, including the Southern Association of Colleges and Schools (SACS), the highly regarded accrediting agency for the Southern states. It remains to this day an important part of American educational literature.

During his 22 years as president of Emmanuel College, Dr. Hopkins led in the most explosive period of growth and expansion in the history of the school. During those years the College achieved the transition from junior college to a four-year liberal arts institution and grew from 300 students to 850 students. He also led in funding and constructing several new buildings on campus. As an ordained minister, he was able to be an effective link between the College and the sponsoring denomination, the International Pentecostal Holiness Church.

Being raised in the home of a pastor, Dr. Hopkins knew the ethos and character of the church firsthand. Always a faithful churchman, he dedicated his life to training future pastors and leaders for the Church. Some of the graduates have become distinguished scholars and pastors of some of the nation's largest megachurches. He also knew about the strengths and weaknesses of his church tradition. One of the strengths of the church was its clear teaching on the *charismata* or gifts of the Spirit. These gifts, including speaking in tongues, healing, and prophecy, have been a major emphasis for which all Pentecostal churches are known.

Over the years, however, the Fruit of the Spirit, which include love, joy, peace, longsuffering, kindness, goodness, faithfulness, gentleness, and self-control (Galatians 5:22-23), have been largely overlooked while many people emphasized the more eye-catching and sometimes sensational gifts of the Spirit. This book is a wonderful attempt to redress this imbalance. In the words of many concerned Christians, "Character still counts" in an age in which seemingly anything goes, even in churches.

I applaud Dr. Hopkins on this very practical excursion into the wonderful and important fruit of the Spirit. As an English major, he is an accomplished writer, a factor which makes the book Nine Habits of Truly Transformed People such a pleasure to read.

Vinson Synan, Ph. D.
Dean of the School of Divinity
Regent University, Virginia Beach, Virginia

ACKNOWLEDGMENTS

In addition to my eternal gratitude to God for the opportunity to write about my abundant and varied life experiences, I want to first of all express my supreme love for my wife, Claudia, and thank her repeatedly for the tremendous source of inspiration, encouragement, and insight she has provided me for almost half a century. In writing about the fruit of the Spirit I have been constantly reminded of the many times in our lives when she, above all, has demonstrated genuine Christlike character in all situations. She has always provided the prayer support and good, sound advice I have needed to stay in the path God has chosen for us together. She is indeed my secret-sharer, my best friend, my constant companion, and my prayer partner. Without her understanding and encouragement I would never have been able to accomplish anything, especially the completion of this book. She is and always has been my secret weapon and source of comfort.

I would also like to thank my children, Chrissie and Mark, both of whom are ministers in their own right, for their input and encouragement as I have pursued this project. Both have made Claudia and me very proud to be their parents, and, along with their spouses and children, they have continued to live consistently the fruit of the Spirit in their lives as well. God also blessed us with a wonderful daughter-in-law, Amy, and kind, generous son-in-law, Jon Forehand, and six grandchildren. No greater wish could be granted.

To my parents, Reverend and Mrs. William Paul Hopkins, I express my deepest appreciation for the examples they set for me in my formative years. Throughout his long, active pastoral ministry my father consistently showed me the fruit of the Spirit in his messages and relationship with the congregations he pastored. Mother has also lived the Christian life in meekness and humility. While Dad has gone to be with the Lord, he has left us a tremendous legacy and example of Christlike character worthy of emulation. Many years ago they gave up worldly possessions and answered the call to ministry regardless of the sacrifices, and they remained true to that calling.

In all my years of working in higher education I have had the privilege of knowing many colleagues who exemplify the qualities this book describes. I think of Dr. C. Y. Melton, my predecessor as president at Emmanuel College; Charles E. Bradshaw, chairman of the Emmanuel College Board of Trustees for many years, with whom I worked closely: Dr. Garnet Pike, a true friend and brother in Christ; Dr. G. Earl Beatty, who served as my executive vice president; Dr. Kirk Hartsfield, who taught me and then served faithfully as one of my administrators for years; Mr. Ed Henson, a uniquely gifted Christian gentlemen about whom many alumni still talk in terms of sainthood; Dr. Don Brady, who has consistently helped me through his gift of laughter; and other truly transformed individuals.

I want to thank Jamie Cain, a very bright young intellect and computer genius, for designing the cover for this book, and Phillip Bowen, Kirk McConnell, Don Collins, and other outstanding young men for their loyalty and decisive leadership. Finally, I want to thank the many friends and colleagues with whom I have worked at Emmanuel College over the past 36 years. From them I have learned much about commitment, sacrifice, and unselfishness. The true test of Christianity is in our relationships, and Emmanuel College has excelled over the years because of the willingness of so many to devote their time and energies to young men and women in their formative years. As a result there are Emmanuel alumni serving faithfully all over the world as they represent Christ and His kingdom. That has made the journey worthwhile.

INTRODUCTION

Read the headlines:

−An angry, frustrated ex-employee who was fired from his job walks into the plant where he had worked and unloads his pistol, killing five workers and his former boss.

−A husband married for 15 years suddenly decides he doesn't want to be married anymore, so he announces to his wife that he wants a divorce.

−A businessman who puts in 80-hour weeks, including Saturdays and Sundays, just to keep up with his associates, wonders why he cannot find any joy in life.

−The CEO of a high-tech computer corporation is indicted for falsifying reports on profits made by the company to deceive stockholders until the company goes bankrupt.

−A prominent U. S. Senator is forced to resign his position of power and authority after accusations of bribery and deception prove to be true.

−Hoping to win the lottery, a worker takes his weekly check and spends it on tickets while his family goes hungry.

−A son, upset because his parents won't give him some money and the use of the car for a Friday night party, kills them both and buries their bodies in the remote woods near his home.

−A college student under pressure by her classmates to party every weekend winds up every Monday with a huge hangover and tries to figure out why her grades are plummeting and she can't feel good about herself.

−A 12-year-old boy who doesn't know who his father is and whose mother deserted him is shuffled from one foster home to another and decides life is not worth living.

−A driver in heavy early morning traffic becomes so enraged when another vehicle cuts in front of him he loses his temper and rear-ends the other car.

−A high school student hooked on drugs gets pregnant and doesn't even remember what happened that night.

Unfortunately the examples of life in the fast lane are endless; bad habits seem to prevail in our society. Something is dreadfully wrong in 21st-century America. In a secular culture that is becoming blatantly anti-Christian, identifying truly transformed people is becoming more and more difficult. Even well-meaning, sincere followers of Christ have swallowed the Hollywood hype and Madison Avenue propaganda about what the good life should be in our country. Words like *commitment*, *dedication*, *values*, *ethics*, and *absolute truth* are becoming obsolete.

Not long ago I came across a quote by Dr. Bob Moorehead from his book, *Words Aptly Spoken*, written in 1995. His insight is profound:

> *The paradox of our time in history is that we have taller buildings but shorter tempers, wider freeways, but narrower viewpoints. We spend more but have less; we buy more, but enjoy less. We have bigger houses and smaller families, more conveniences, but less time. We have more degrees but less sense; more knowledge, but less judgment; more experts, yet more problems; more medicine, but less wellness.*
>
> *We drink too much, smoke too much, spend too recklessly, laugh too little, drive too fast, get too angry, stay up too late, get up too tired, read too little, watch TV too much, and pray too seldom. We have multiplied our possessions, but reduced our values. We talk too much, love too seldom, and hate too often.*
>
> *We've learned how to make a living, but not a life. We've added years to life but not life to years. We've been all the way to the moon and back, but have trouble crossing the street to meet a new neighbor. We conquered outer space but not inner space. We've done larger things, but not better things.*
>
> *We've cleaned up the air, but polluted the soul. We've conquered the atom, but not our prejudice. We write more, but learn less. We plan more, but accomplish less. We've learned to rush, but not to wait. We build more computers to hold more information, to produce more copies than ever, but we communicate less and less.*
>
> *These are the times of fast foods and slow digestion, big men and small character, steep profits and shallow relationships. These are the days of two incomes but more divorce, fancier houses, but broken homes. These are days of quick trips, disposable diapers, throwaway morality, one night stands, overweight bodies, and pills that do everything for cheer, to quiet, to kill. It is a time when there is much in the showroom window and nothing in the stockroom. A time when technology can bring this letter to you, and a time when you can choose either to share this insight, or to just hit delete.*[1]

Wow! I don't think anyone could have summarized our society better! Knowing what to believe and how to respond to the pressures of life is becoming a major challenge for Christians. After all, from the media, including news editorials, talk shows on TV, and even movies on TV and in the theaters, we keep hearing statements like these: "It doesn't matter what you believe as long as you're sincere"; "In a multicultural, democratic society we need to embrace all alternate lifestyles as equal"; "Whatever god a person believes in is okay because god is just a symbol"; and "Truth is relative; what may be wrong in one situation may be right in another." Anyway, you get the picture. It appears that Christianity is becoming the real alternative lifestyle. Anyone professing to live according to the teachings and beliefs of Jesus is branded as a fanatic, radical conservative, and bigot.

In their book *How Now Shall We Live?*, Charles Colson and Nancy Pearcey state,

> "We live in a culture that is at best morally indifferent. A culture in which Judeo-Christian values are mocked and where immorality in high places is not only ignored but even rewarded in the voting booth. A culture in which violence, banality, meanness, and disintegrating personal behavior are destroying civility and endangering the very life of our communities. A culture in which the most profound moral dilemmas are addressed by the cold logic of utilitarianism."[2]

They continue,

> "What's more, when Christians do make good-faith efforts to halt the slide into barbarism, we are maligned as intolerant or bigoted. Small wonder that many people have concluded that the "culture war" is over—and that we have lost. Battle weary, we are tempted to withdraw into the safety of our sanctuaries, to keep busy by plugging into every program offered by our megachurches, hoping to keep ourselves and our children safe from the coming desolation."[3]

Indeed, we are creatures of habit. Before one knows it, one is engulfed in a dilemma about what should be the proper lifestyle and daily behavior for a person wishing to please God. Again, even church-going Christians with good intentions become absorbed into a culture that is largely corrupted by

Satan and filled with pitfalls. Understanding the lifestyle that pleases God and emulates Christ in such a perverse society is becoming a daily challenge for anyone desiring to live as a Christian. *Where do I draw the line? What is acceptable behavior and what is not? Do I gauge my behavior by what I see other Christians doing? How can I be a Christian without being ridiculed and rejected by my peers?* I hope this study will help to answer these and other questions about how to develop the habits of Christlike character.

Then another dilemma for those who are trying to find and live Christianity is the confusion among Christians themselves over denominations, styles of worship, music, the megachurch movement, and other aspects of living that bring questions of spirituality and fitness for the kingdom. Who is right and who is wrong? On the one hand Pentecostal and charismatic Christians flock to a more demonstrative, performance style of worship with prophetic ministry and gifts of the Spirit manifested in the service, while other denominations prefer a more sedate, traditional type of worship. Congregations of thousands are springing up in cities across the country, while many Christians still attend small rural churches that remain basically the same in size and style of worship as they have for many years. Where is true Christianity to be found in all the variations of the Church?

Another problem for non-Christians is the fact that Christians in local churches don't seem to be able to get along. Almost every day we read or hear of another church split over some ridiculous argument like the color of the carpet or the type of music to be emphasized in worship. Habits like jealousy, envy, pride, arrogance, and bitterness too easily creep into the congregation and cause all kinds of disruption and corruption. Professing Christians just don't get it. Nothing could be further from the model Christ exemplified for the Church.

Again, Colson and Pearcey write,

> "The church's singular failure in recent decades has been the failure to see Christianity as a life system, or worldview, that governs every area of existence. This failure has been crippling in many ways. For one thing, we cannot answer the questions our children bring home from school, so we are incapable of preparing them to answer the challenges they face. For ourselves, we cannot explain to our friends and neighbors why we believe, and we often cannot defend our faith. And we do not know how to organize our lives correctly, allowing

our choices to be shaped by the world around us. What's more, by failing to see Christian truth in every aspect of life, we miss great depths of beauty and meaning: the thrill of seeing God's splendor in the intricacies of nature or hearing his voice in the performance of a great symphony or detecting his character in the harmony of a well-ordered community."[4]

Where is the solution to be found? The answer to the question of achieving a Christian lifestyle, I believe, is to be found in getting back to the basics of the Bible. Examining the life and teachings of Jesus separates the essential from the extraneous, the requirements from the optional. One thing that all Christians must agree upon is that certain behavioral characteristics must be evident in the life of a believer in Christ or the world will not pay attention. For true Christianity to be effective, what happens outside the walls of the sanctuary is far more significant than what takes place in the Sunday morning service! That is where Christlike living must be the common denominator for followers of Christ.

A Need for Understanding

Now, before I become too absorbed in passionate discourse about today's dilemma, let me explain how this study came to be. For a number of years I have been teaching and reading about the Fruit of the Spirit (listed in Galatians 5:22 and 23) as characteristics of the Christian's walk with God. I believe many people lack an understanding of just what makes the Christian life different from any other culture, religion, or lifestyle on earth and need some simple clarification of the real difference that occurs in one's life once he embraces Christ as Savior and Lord. Without a doubt, what Jesus lived and taught is vastly removed from any other philosophy, religion, or perspective presented by any human being before or since His coming to earth, and once a person grasps the enormity of that distinctiveness, as presented in the words and actions of Jesus Himself, his or her life will never be the same. Through the transforming power of the Holy Spirit, one is capable of developing a lifestyle consisting of holy, healthy habits as demonstrated by Jesus Himself.

Following Christ's example is the key. In the Fruit of the Spirit are found the answers to the mysteries of the kingdom of God, and putting into practice the behavior exemplified in these characteristics of Christ brings fulfillment, meaning, and eternal significance to one's life. As a method of presenting each of the characteristics of Christ listed as the Fruit of the Spirit in Galatians 5:22 and 23, this study first gives a precise, concrete definition of each and then explains the meaning of key words and/or phrases of that definition. The discussion is further enhanced by scriptural references and examples as well as personal illustrations from the author's life. Hopefully this method will prove to be simple and inspirational for the reader.

The Struggle Between Works and Grace

One more point must be made here. There are so many conflicting, confusing philosophies and theologies being promoted in 21st-century America, maybe a clear, simple, systematic explanation of the type of behavior made possible by the power of the Holy Spirit will change some perspectives and even lives. We human beings are so limited in our ability to understand the power of God to bring about change, we repeatedly try to substitute other aspects of our existence for God's infinite wisdom and grace.

A familiar dilemma for Christians is the attempt to replace the miraculous transformation that takes place in the life of a person who submits his or her life to Christ with our own human efforts to work our way to heaven, and non-Christians have a difficult time understanding what happens when an individual gives his life to Christ. As human beings we are torn between our own efforts to make it to heaven and simply allowing the Holy Spirit to transform us into the image of Christ. Thankfully, who I am does not depend upon what I do or what others might think of my performance in a job or particular role. The essential difference between a Christian and non-Christian must be intrinsic; what happens by faith when a person believes on Jesus Christ is not to be comprehended by our finite minds. It is a miracle of God performed by the Holy Spirit. When that transformation happens, God begins to change us and shape us into the type of vessel He can use to transform others.

The Fruit of the Spirit is produced supernaturally when a person confesses Christ as Savior and Lord of his life. As he continues to submit his life to Christ, grows spiritually through prayer and study of God's Word, and is obedient to the Holy Spirit, he begins to operate in the power of God that puts within him a desire to be like Jesus. Then the Fruit of the Spirit begins to be evident in his behavior and relationships with God and others.

It is that transformation which differentiates a Christian from any other person. Only when a person is truly transformed by the power of the Holy Spirit can he or she begin to demonstrate a Christlike character. That is the distinctiveness Christ exemplified and taught during His earthly life. And that is the character of a Christian produced as the Fruit of the Spirit.

No Fulfillment Without Fruit

Now what this study is attempting to accomplish is to define, explain, and clarify in concrete terms what each of the nine Fruit of the Spirit listed in Galatians 5:22 and 23 means in the life of a Christian and how one may be more aware of the continuous, simultaneous development of the Fruit of the Spirit in his or her life as Christian maturity occurs. Jesus, for example, stated, *Just as I have loved you, you must love one another. This is how all men will know that you are my disciples, because you have such love for one another* (John 13:35, Phillips). What the Fruit of the Spirit accomplishes is to transform a person into the kind of human being God wants him to become to make the kingdom of God a reality on earth. It is this kind of relationship and behavior that causes the world to sit up and take notice. It is this kind of lifestyle that speaks loudly to a secular world and says, "God has changed my life, and I am striving first and foremost to be like Jesus in everything I do."

Indeed, Christianity lived out in the world is the most radically different lifestyle observable. After all, a person who has been miraculously transformed into a child of God really understands for the first time that this earthly life is just a prelude to eternal life in heaven and that our role in this world is to glorify God through emulating the life and teachings of Jesus. In other words, the kingdom of God is advanced through those who represent Christ and carry out the Great Commission. This life, simply, is "on-the-job" training for the glorious, endless joy of experiencing eternity in heaven. One who truly allows the Fruit of the Spirit to develop in his or her life does not have to try to manipulate, perform, or attempt to be a Christian. There is no way we can work out our own salvation and eternal joy. The love, joy, peace, patience, kindness, goodness, meekness, faithfulness, and self-control produced by the Holy Spirit will be so evident in the life of a believer the world will quickly notice him. The results of a person's living for Christ as demonstrated by the Fruit of the Spirit working in his actions will be so radically different from the typical lifestyle of the world he or she won't have to say anything. The difference will prompt a non-Christian to say, "I don't know what that guy has in his life to bring about such faith and joy, but I want to find out so I can have it too."

A Personal Journey

The idea for this study actually comes from many years of teaching, studying, and observing human behavior from a Christian perspective. You see, I grew up in a pastor's home and have formulated my beliefs and convictions from a very early age. During my formative years I spent numerous hours each week in church at one function or another. This was a part of our lives; there was no question about church involvement. We just went! As a result of these experiences, I have a lifetime of memories and observations to make about what I think the essentials of Christian living are. As a preacher's kid I probably heard too much and learned a great deal about the imperfections of all of us. The obvious shortcomings and foibles of church members gave a young boy reason to assess the whole situation of being a Christian and determine in his heart what was important. My inquisitive mind said, "Surely there is more to life than the superficial display of anger, resentment, jealousy, greed, and bitterness I see evident in the lives of some people, even church members." These factors initially led to my search for the real Christianity.

Of course, as I grew up, I "got saved" many times. Going to the altar on Sunday night became a ritual because I knew my parents were watching me to see if I was really religious. The problem was that no one really ever explained to me what the real transformation is when one becomes a Christian. I knew that there were certain things Christians didn't do (like smoke, drink, curse, go to movies, etc.), but reasons behind actions were not clear. Understanding why Christians were different was not taught in a simple, systematic way to accentuate the positive power the Holy Spirit brings to one's life when he or she is transformed and made a "new creation." Too often in my maturation process the focus in the church was upon instantaneous crisis experiences like "getting saved, sanctified, and filled with the Holy Ghost," and explanations of how to live like Christ were few and far between. The obvious inconsistencies in the lives of those who professed to be Christians also brought confusion and questions.

Even as a young adult, I still wrestled with the entire question of Christianity and the choices one makes in life as a believer or non-believer. How to separate the essentials from the extraneous in serving Christ was difficult for a young person to grasp, and I continued to ponder the dilemma of living like Christ in a world that increasingly offered opposite alternatives. I had yet to discover the writings of men like C. S. Lewis, Francis Schaeffer, Charles Colson, and others who have had a profound influence upon my thinking, and no one in the church seemed to be able to present didactically the gospel in a way that would encourage a young Christian to follow Christ.

Then, largely because of my desire to learn, I determined that I was going to study as much as possible to be able to serve the Lord to the maximum extent. Therefore, I spent many years completing undergraduate and graduate degrees. During this process of attending both Christian and secular colleges, I further gained valuable insight regarding both the Christian and secular worldviews. Because of my own journey to the acquisition of knowledge, I have always been a proponent of higher education, especially Christian education. There is no substitute for formal training for those who are searching for answers and who would choose to be of utmost benefit to the cause of Christ.

Finally, for 43 years I have been actively involved in education, from the classroom to academic deanship to the presidency of a Christian college for 22 years. I have a world of memories of relationships with colleagues, students, parents, board members, alumni, and public officials whose lives have profoundly affected mine. Again, because of dealing with human beings of all ages in a variety of situations and observing that we are "all sinners saved by grace," I wanted to provide a simple volume of instruction and inspiration for those who are genuinely seeking to be like Jesus, to find the source of meaning in life, and to live victoriously as Christians.

Further, having mentored, taught, and encouraged thousands of young college students through the years, I especially wanted to provide a clear guide to assist young Christians in their quest for the real Jesus. I have a feeling that many of our younger generation are genuinely searching for help as they face the complexities and uncertainties of an increasingly indifferent, ambiguous society. I also suspect that they are not getting clear, definitive answers from the church to their questions about the essential aspects of a Christian life. As the world and the United States of America plummet dangerously downward toward destruction, the lines are being drawn more certainly between Christianity and secularism or downright blatant anti-Christian movements. Thus, it is absolutely essential that truly transformed Christians take a stand and follow the habits of Christlike behavior regardless of the consequences. Old habits are hard to break. It takes a miraculous intervention and transformation for a person to strive for Christlike character. Furthermore, in order for a truly transformed Christian to be salt and light in this world, there must be a life of daily prayer, study of God's Word, and communication with Him. That is the challenge ahead and the salvation for the world!

David R. Hopkins

CHAPTER ONE

How To Develop Habits Of Christlike Character

John 1:1-2, 10-12 – *In the beginning was the Word, and the Word was with God, and the Word was God. The same was in the beginning with God. . . He was in the world, and the world was made by him, and the world knew him not. He came unto his own, and own received him not. But as many as received him, to them gave he power to become the sons of God, even to them that believe on his name* (KJV).

"Now is our chance to choose the right side. God is holding back to give us a choice. It won't last forever. We must take it or leave it."
C. S. Lewis, *The Case for Christianity*

Is There a Character Gap in Christianity?

True Christianity as exemplified through Christlike character is difficult to recognize the in 21st century. Too many times a huge gap exists between what we Christians say we believe and how we decide to respond to our culture and society. Rather than simply relying upon what Christ taught and lived, many sincere people are turning to other sources for instruction and inspiration. In the information age there are numerous self-styled gurus and soothsayers who claim to know how to instruct us on the proper way to be happy in this post-Christian era. With the affluence and availability of all sorts of material benefits in America, people are still desperately seeking for meaning and substance to ease the guilt and pain of separation from God. They are really searching for the love, joy, peace, patience, kindness, meekness, goodness, faithfulness, and self-control produced only through a transformed life but don't know how to find true meaning in life. The writer C. S. Lewis, said, "Human beings, all over the earth, have this curious idea that they ought to behave in a certain way, and can't really get rid of it."[1] God has put within every person the capability and desire to be like Him.

In a modern parody similar to Lewis's ***Screwtape Letters,*** I recently read this illustration:

Satan called a worldwide convention. In his opening address to his evil angels, he said, "We can't keep the Christians from going to church. We can't keep them from reading their Bibles and knowing the truth. We can't even keep them from forming an intimate, abiding relationship experience in Christ. If they gain that connection with Jesus, our power over them is broken. So let them go to their churches; let them have their conservative lifestyles, but steal their time, so they can't gain that relationship with Jesus Christ. This is what I want you to do, angels. Distract them from gaining hold on their Savior and maintaining that vital connection throughout their day!"

"How shall we do this?" shouted his angels.

"Keep them busy in the nonessentials of life and invent innumerable schemes to occupy their minds," he answered. "Tempt them to spend, spend, spend, and borrow, borrow, borrow. Persuade the wives to go to work for long hours and the husbands to work six or seven days each week, 10-12 hours a day, so they can afford their empty lifestyles. Keep them from spending time with their children. As their family fragments, soon their home will offer no escape from the pressures of work. Overstimulate their minds so that they cannot hear that still, small voice. Entice them to play the radio or cassette player whenever they drive. To keep the TV, VCR, CDs, and their PCs going constantly in their home and see to it that every store and restaurant in the world plays non-biblical music constantly. This will jam their minds and break that union with Christ.

"Fill the coffee tables with magazines and newspapers. Pound their minds with the news 24 hours a day. Invade their driving

moments with billboards. Flood their mailboxes with junk mail, mail-order catalogs, sweepstakes, and every kind of newsletter and promotional offering free products, services, and false hopes. Keep skinny, beautiful models on the magazines so the husbands will believe that external beauty is what's important, and they'll become dissatisfied with their wives. Ha! That will fragment those families quickly.

"Even in their recreation, let them be excessive. Have them return from their recreation exhausted, disquieted, and unprepared for the coming week. Don't let them go out in nature to reflect on God's wonders. Send them to amusement parks, sporting events, concerts, and movies instead. Keep them busy, busy, busy! And when they meet for spiritual fellowship, involve them in gossip and small talk so that they leave with troubled consciences and unsettled emotions. Go ahead, let them be involved in soul winning; but crowd their lives with so many good causes they have no time to seek power from Jesus. Soon they will be working on their own strength, sacrificing their health and family for the good of the cause. It will work! It will work!"

It was quite a convention. The evil angels went eagerly to their assignments causing Christians everywhere to get more busy and more rushed, going here and there. I guess the question is: "Has the devil been successful at his scheme?"[2]

In our high-intensity, fast-fleeting daily activities, we have become so busy we forget the most important purpose in life. As Jesus taught in the parable of the treasure found in the field, once a person finds the kingdom of God, everything else pales into nothingness. Suddenly one's total purpose and perspective of life drastically change. The genuine transformation that takes place when a person grasps the scope of God's redemptive power changes his entire focus. Like suddenly finding a valuable treasure beyond comprehension, the newborn Christian is ready to sell everything he has to possess Christ. That is when Christlike character begins. That is when a person turns his attention and devotion to prayer, studying scriptures, and reading daily from inspiring books, magazines, or on-line materials that will build his faith and character. This habitual devotion and worship leads to spiritual growth and the growth of the Fruit of the Spirit in one's life.

The problem, from this writer's perspective, is that Christians too often are so captivated by a self-centered, materialistic society's demands and are so busy trying to live dual, conflicting lives, they are not certain about their eternal place in God's plan. What is needed is a thorough, personal assessment of our priorities from the one essential source – the life and example of Jesus Christ Himself. After all, He provided the plan and taught clearly the values and qualities one needs to possess to be His servant. These characteristics of Christ are listed in several places in the New Testament and are often referred to as the "Fruit of the Spirit." An understanding of what these qualities are and how they may be operative in the life of a believer is essential to be as effective as possible as a Christian in this world. Thus, this study attempts to identify and define specifically what the "Fruit of the Spirit" may add to the life of a Christian and what we may do to live the abundant life Christ offers.

Our Habits Illustrate Who We are

One may wonder about the choice of title for this study. Obviously, this writer has read and admired Stephen Covey's brilliant book entitled *The Seven Habits of Highly Effective People: Powerful Lessons in Personal Change*, a volume that has profoundly affected the business world in a positive way by pointing out a number of principles to apply to one's personal life, work ethic, and corporate behavior.[3] He integrates certain "character ethics" into one's development of a successful life, and focuses upon definite principles of behavior that govern our decision-making. The clarity and simplicity of Covey's approach influenced my thinking about how to present the supernatural transformation that takes place when a person submits his or her life to Christ and starts on the road to emulating His life and teachings. After all, if there can be such truth to be found in applying certain principles to one's business relationships and behavior, how much more important is it that we understand the real essentials of becoming successful Christians in a secular society?

Admittedly, the use of the word *habit* to describe the development of Christlike behavior in one's life might be troublesome to some readers, but a habit is something we do automatically, without even realizing we are doing it on most occasions. We are, in fact, what we do repeatedly, whether we realize it or not. A habit becomes second nature and is an act performed without calculation or thinking about whether or not the results are good or bad. Stephen Covey defines a habit as "the intersection of *knowledge, skill, and desire.*"[4] He clarifies, "Knowledge is the theoretical paradigm, the *what to do* and the *why*. Skill is the *how to do*. And desire is the motivation, the *want to do*. In order to make something a habit in our lives, we have to have all three."[5] In the realm of holy habits (Fruit of the Spirit) certainly there must be *knowledge*. One must know the Word of God and make the words of Jesus part of his daily life in order to understand the concept of bearing fruit. Then part of a habit is, of course, *skill*. In other words, there must be some action or behavior that is consistent and subconscious to demonstrate that a person has actually made a certain belief or principle part of his lifestyle. The old axiom says, "Practice makes perfect," and that is true of exercising the Fruit of the Spirit in our lives as well. Then *desire* is supernaturally provided to the regenerated person by the power of the Holy Spirit working in the life as one strives to be like Jesus. Therefore, Covey's definition of a "habit" applies to the Christian's development of the qualities defined as the Fruit of the Spirit.

Let me illustrate. In His parable of the separation of the sheep and goats in Matthew 25:32-46, Jesus points out that the sheep didn't realize they were acting in a way that would please God and distinguish them from the goats. Those chosen to inherit the Kingdom responded to life's situations the way Jesus would. They gave water to the thirsty, clothed the naked, comforted the stranger, ministered to the sick, and helped the prisoners just because that was what Christians do. They didn't intentionally do so but said, "Lord, when did we do these things?" In other words, the Fruit of the Spirit worked automatically in their lives as they followed Christ. Thus, they developed the habit of being like Christ.

C. S. Lewis put it this way: "Your natural life is derived from your parents; that does not mean it will stay there if you do nothing about it. You can lose it by neglect, or you can drive it away by committing suicide. You have to feed it and look after it; but always remember you are not making it, you are only keeping up a life you got from someone else. In the same way a Christian can lose the Christ-life which has been put into him, and he has to make efforts to keep it. But even the best Christian that ever lived is not acting on his own steam—he is only nourishing or protecting a life he could never have acquired by his own efforts."[6]

The premise of this study, then, is that God transforms a life through the supernatural power of the Holy Spirit, and when man becomes a "new creation," he has the potential to develop all the character traits Christ exemplified during His earthly life. Thus, love, joy, peace, patience, and the other characteristics that make up the "Fruit of the Spirit" may be (indeed, must be) present and evident in the life of a Christian.

Jesus Said, "Learn of Me"

The next step, then, would be for one who has submitted his or her life to Christ to be able to understand these nine essential traits or habits that should be simultaneously evident in a Christian's behavior. The essence of Christianity is internal and supernatural. In other words, the world's perception of who we are is determined by the character of Christ demonstrated in our daily behavior throughout life. For many years (22 years as a Christian college president and 43 years in education) I have studied human behavior and especially the unique distinctiveness that makes a Christian effective in his or her witness. My observations have led me to believe that, in many instances, we Christians have focused our attention more upon the "Gifts of the Spirit" and have emphasized works. At the same time we have neglected to seek understanding of the most important aspect of Christianity – becoming more like Christ.

Another observation at this point is that we Christians tend to focus our attention and spiritual aspirations more upon obtaining the "Gifts of the Spirit" than upon understanding and living the "Fruit of the Spirit." Check, for example, the list of books, articles, and lessons written about knowing, acquiring, and using the "Gifts of the Spirit" compared to those discussing and clarifying the "Fruit of the Spirit." Obviously exercising the Gifts of the Spirit in the Body of Christ is exciting, demonstrative, and impressive, but a Christian may be very limited in his or her possession and performance of the Gifts of the Spirit. On the other hand, it is possible for one to exhibit God-given gifts without very much evidence of character development in his life. However, the Fruit of the Spirit must be evident in the life of every believer, or something is dreadfully wrong with our connection to Christ. In other words, the Gifts are optional. Fruit is essential.

After all, Christ's concepts are simple and clear. The path of victorious Christian living is laid out repeatedly in His teachings; yet the evidence is not widely apparent that those who claim to be Christians fully grasp the significance of certain centralities of living, the distinctive traits that truly change a person forever. Those attributes supernaturally developed through an abiding relationship with Christ are listed in various places in the Bible, especially in the Gospels, and Jesus repeatedly tried to get His listeners to understand the tremendous differences brought about by following Him. These distinctive characteristics are often categorized as "the Fruit of the Spirit."

A Matter of Semantics

I must insert here that my educational training was in linguistics and the study of the English language. From a very young age I loved reading and analyzing the structure of the oral and written communication God has so perfectly created for us. My fascination with the language has led me to more specific study of words and meanings as we struggle to translate abstract concepts into concrete definitions. You see, the English language is not as precise and direct as some other languages in leading us to a more specific understanding of certain ideas.

For example, the simple word *love* in English has so many different possibilities of interpretation that one has to become familiar with the context and the concept behind a particular use of the word in a sentence. Look up the word *love* in the English dictionary, and there will be numerous definitions from which to choose dependent upon the context. However, other languages are more focused. Greek, for example, had a number of words that described different meanings of what we generally call "love." There was a different word for fraternal (*phileo*), paternal (*storge*), romantic or carnal (*eros*), and divine love (*agape*). Therefore, in reading the New Testament in the original Greek, one could readily identify the meaning of a particular passage. The Greek word *agape* was used when reference was made to the distinctive supernatural love God has for His creation. That is the context for Paul's wonderful and meaningful definition of love in I Corinthians 13.

Precise Definitions Needed

Now, because the English language is so abstract in identifying meanings for the understanding of the reader or listener, it is important that we have some clarification or interpretation of terms that are not easily explained. In this study I am attempting to do just that. Of course, I readily draw upon the writings of others, like the outstanding teachings of Bill Gothard, who attempted to do the same thing. Gothard, for one, has been a great mentor of many through his multitudinous materials related to all kinds of aspects of Christian living. His definitions, illustrations, and examples have been an inspiration to me and have offered clarity and conciseness to all of us. (For further instruction from Gothard's teaching on discipleship and character, go to www.billgothard.com.)

On the other hand, I have not found many extensive discussions focused primarily on the distinctive nature of each of the Fruit of the Spirit, the unique aspects of each term listed in Galatians 5:22 and 23, II Peter 1:5-7, II Timothy 3:10, and other New Testament passages devoted to listing these qualities. I should clarify at this juncture, also, that the singular term "Fruit," not the plural "Fruits," is used when describing the totality of the qualities Christ represented (such as love, joy, peace, longsuffering, etc.) because these virtues are evident and inseparable as they are present in the life of a Christian. Together they comprise the "Fruit" of the Spirit as the follower of Christ allows the Holy Spirit to work in his or her life, developing simultaneously the various components of a Christlike character. Some writers have suggested that the nine graces or virtues that comprise the Fruit of the Spirit may be divided into three groups of three. The first three (Love, Joy, Peace) are actions toward God; the second three (Patience, Kindness, Goodness) are actions toward our fellowmen; and the final three (Faithfulness, Meekness, Self-Control) are related to our self-improvement. In other words, none of these qualities works independently of the others. Indeed, they complement and enhance each other throughout our Christian journey as we seek to truly be like Christ. A person who is led by the Holy Spirit will produce all nine of the Fruit of the Spirit!

Now, without belaboring the point, my thesis in this discussion is to clarify for the reader each of the nine Fruit of the Spirit listed in Galatians 5:22 and 23 by defining more concretely the meaning of each and by describing in detail how each is identified. I should also quickly state that the discussions of these characteristics are not meant to be prescriptive but descriptive. In other words, there is no mechanical or technical way to acquire the Fruit of the Spirit. I cannot wake up one day and say, "Well, today I'm going to concentrate on 'joy' or 'kindness' or 'meekness.'" Fruit doesn't just happen. The production of fruit in our lives doesn't come from intellect, endeavor, or ingenuity. Fruit on the tree or vine is produced simply by abiding, being attached to the source of nourishment and life. The apple, peach, or plum doesn't work to reach maturity; it simply waits and ripens as the tree gives it life. After all, in John 15:5 Jesus very directly says, *I am the vine, ye are the branches: He that abideth in me, and I in him, the same bringeth forth much fruit: for without me ye can do nothing* (KJV).

In conclusion, I believe many Christians are desperately looking for answers in a world of sin, corruption, and deception. Where is the truth to be found? How can I find Christ amid all the vanity, selfishness, and confusion around me? If I am truly living my life to emulate Christ, how is that possible? Where is the genuine to be found in the midst of all the artificial, fake, and hypocritical in the world? The answers to these and other questions the serious seeker is asking, I believe, are to be found first of all in truly establishing a personal, intimate relationship with Jesus Christ and then spending a lifetime endeavoring to understand the meaning of "Christ in you, the hope of glory." As Christ's personality becomes a part of our thinking, living, and being, we will automatically begin to demonstrate the Fruit of the Spirit in our everyday behavior, but I think it is important that we study the characteristics of the Fruit of the Spirit to be able to identify these essential qualities as they are developed in us. I have found this kind of study of the individual concepts of love, joy, peace, longsuffering, gentleness or kindness, goodness, faithfulness, meekness, and self-control to be invaluable in my desire to know Christ better, and I hope you will, too.

Amid the cacophony of chaotic daily confusion,
Lord, come and fill me with your presence and power
To become a valid vessel chosen for the Kingdom.
Let me not forget the vine and the branches
Where You produce life-giving and life-changing transformation
To all who will believe and receive your authority and dominion.
As the healthy tree effortlessly grows the sweet, succulent fruit,
I will rest in your unchanging, unrelenting grace and mature!
Feed me, Holy Spirit, from your everlasting flow
Of nourishing, nurturing power to change,
And I will live my life in the wisdom and eternal assurance of
divine love.

CHAPTER TWO

The Fruit And The Tree: The Principle Of Fruit-bearing

John 15:5—I am the Vine, you are the branches. When you're joined with me and I with you, the relation intimate and organic, the harvest is sure to be abundant. Separated, you can't produce a thing (Msg).

When I was a boy, we were visiting my grandmother's house in Danville, Virginia. I was always hungry, and when I saw a basket of fruit on the dining room table, I immediately grabbed an apple and bit into it. Much to my surprise I actually tasted plastic instead of the real thing. The fruit looked so real I did not recognize that it was simply imitation. Unfortunately, life is that way.

Warning! You cannot develop healthy, holy habits alone. Becoming a fruit-bearing person doesn't just happen. One cannot within himself ever habitually love as Jesus loved, express the joy of the Lord in his life, or experience any other Fruit of the Spirit. Simply put, as Christ Himself illustrated, no branch is going to produce fruit unless it is attached to the vine rooted into the ground from which its nourishment comes. Jesus pointed this out. He said, *I am the vine; you are the branches. He that abideth in me and I in him, the same bringeth forth much fruit: for without me you can do nothing* (KJV). In fact, the first eight verses of John 15 complete Christ's very effective illustration solidifying the fact that He is the source of any fruit-bearing that may come for a Christian. His purpose in coming to earth was to be the "true vine," the only way a human being may find real peace and purpose in life. Through abiding in the vine, Christ said, one may produce fruit, *more* fruit, and *much* fruit (note the progression in John 15:1-8). The secret to success from a Christian perspective is to abide in the vine. Therefore, *If you abide in me, and my words abide in you, you shall ask what you will and it shall be done unto you* (John 15:7, KJV), Jesus remarked. In other words, the whole Christian life revolves around being connected to the source of supernatural power and strength – Jesus Christ. The Christian life is fulfilling through *trusting*, not *trying*.

Galatians 5:22 and 23 present a simple, succinct list of qualities identified as Fruit of the Spirit. However, throughout the Bible are to be found illustrations, analogies, and references to the life-giving properties of the tree or vine. The first Psalm describes the parallel between a godly man and a tree. *And he shall be like a tree planted by the rivers of water, that bringeth forth his fruit in his season; his leaf also shall not wither; and whatsoever he doeth shall prosper* (Psalm 1:3, KJV). In Jeremiah 17:5-8 the writer uses a similar description, contrasting the man who puts his trust in God with the man who trusts in the law or in other men. He emphasizes that the man who trusts and hopes in the Lord is like a tree planted by the river drawing constant nourishment from the water, never ceasing to yield fruit.

In addition, Psalm 92 describes the contrast between grass which soon perishes (v. 7) and the palm tree and cedar trees which enjoy long and fruitful lives (vs. 12-14). The man who delights in and meditates upon God's Word, who trusts in God, and who has been enlightened by God will always bear fruit. Then in Matthew 3:10 John the Baptist reiterated this image with reference to the hypocrisy of the Pharisees and Sadducees: *Every tree which bringeth not forth good fruit is hewn down, and cast into the fire.* Note, also, the references of Jesus Himself in the Sermon on the Mount. In Matthew 7:15-20 He speaks of false teachers by using the illustration of fruit-bearing trees: *Beware of false prophets, which come to you in sheep's clothing, but inwardly they are ravening wolves. Ye shall know them by their fruits. Do men gather grapes of thorns, or figs of thistles? Even so every good tree bringeth forth good fruit; but a corrupt tree bringeth forth evil fruit. A good tree cannot bring forth evil fruit, neither can a corrupt tree bring forth good fruit. Every tree that bringeth not forth good fruit is hewn down, and cast into the fire. Wherefore by their fruits ye shall know them* (KJV).

Bearing Fruit Is Essential

In other words, Christ's teaching takes Christianity out of the realm of mere ethics and identifies it as not just a "way of life," but life itself. Fruit, then, is not something that can be transferred or super-imposed by any external means. Developing Christlike character is not the same as learning good habits, such as those which a parent develops in his child. Neither is it a set of rules and behavior brought about through discipline, such as those in the military experience. Producing fruit is the direct result of a work performed in a person's spirit and soul by an immediate supernatural operation of God!

Then the words of Jesus in John 12:24-26 bring closure to the entire matter of how the Fruit of the Spirit operates in one's life. Here He states, *I tell you truly that unless a grain of wheat falls into the earth and dies, it remains a single grain of wheat; but if it dies, it brings a good harvest. The man who loves his own life will destroy it, and the man who hates his life in this world will preserve it for eternal life. If a man wants to enter my service, he must follow my way; and where I am, my servant will also be. And my Father will honor every man who enters my service* (Phillips). In other words, before abundant life in the Spirit may occur, there has to be a death of the previous life, attitudes, perceptions, and habits. In his book *Mere Christianity,* C. S. Lewis points out, "Until you have given up yourself to Him you will not have a real self."[1] One's entire outlook, spirit, and focus must be changed by the Holy Spirit in order for that person to be productive in the kingdom of God. There must be a death in order to bring a fruitful life. That is where the miraculous "new birth" and "new creation" Jesus talked about happen to a person who confesses Christ as Savior and Lord of his life. From that moment on, a tremendous transformation begins to take place. The entire motivation, actions, and attitudes of a Christian begin to be shaped by his or her submission to Christ and obedience to His will. That is why Paul said, "I am crucified with Christ," "I die daily," "Not I but Christ in me," and other proclamations in his letters. And that is when the Fruit of the Spirit begins to manifest itself in everything the Christian does.

Now Paul in his writings gives plenty of specific examples of the fruitful life and the unfruitful life. Galatians 5:22 and 23 are not the only listing of examples of the qualities expected of a Christian as exemplified by Christ. In Romans 5:3-5 he mentions hope, patience, and love. In I Timothy 6:11

another list includes righteousness, godliness, faith, love, patience, and meekness. Still another reference is II Timothy 3:10, where he lists manner of life (conduct), purpose, faith, longsuffering, charity (love), and patience. Isn't it interesting that every list includes "longsuffering" or "patience"? Obviously patience is one of the most important aspects of the Fruit to be developed in the Christian's life. We can all say "Amen!" to that.

Giving further clarity to Christ's supernatural work in man, Peter also speaks under the anointing in II Peter 1:3-7, where he says, *He has by his own action given us everything that is necessary for living the truly good life, in allowing us to know the one who has called us to him, through his own glorious goodness. It is through him that God's greatest and most precious promises have become available to us men, making it possible for you to escape the inevitable disintegration that lust produces in the world and to share God's essential nature. For this very reason you must do your utmost from your side, and see that your faith carries with it real goodness of life. Your goodness must be accompanied by knowledge, your knowledge by self-control, your self-control by the ability to endure. Your endurance too must always be accompanied by a real trust in God; that in turn must have in it the quality of brotherliness, and your brotherliness must lead on to Christian love* (Phillips). The reader readily notices the simultaneous, yet progressive, listing of evidences of the Christian life Peter includes in this passage. Yes, the Fruit of the Spirit comes through the supernatural power of the Holy Spirit, but the Christian must be aware of his part in seeing that these qualities are operating in his life. Walking with Christ is a covenant relationship between a man and Christ that demands total allegiance and commitment.

Then Peter very clearly goes on to state, *If you have these qualities existing and growing in you then it means that knowing our Lord Jesus Christ has not made your lives either complacent or unproductive. The man whose life fails to exhibit these qualities is shortsighted—he can no longer see the reason why he was cleansed from his former sins. Set your minds, then, on endorsing by your conduct the fact that God has called and chosen you. If you go along the lines I have indicated above, there is no reason why you should stumble, and if you have lived the sort of life I have recommended God will open wide to you the gates of the eternal kingdom of our Lord and Savior, Jesus Christ* (II Peter 8-11, Phillips). Again, a consciousness of the operation of the Holy Spirit in one's life is essential to maximum productivity of fruit and living a Christlike life.

Bad Habits Must Be Changed Supernaturally

Now before we leave this discussion, we also need to point out that Paul gets specific in listing some of the results of a non-Christian life that manifest themselves through ignorance and defiance of God's will and purpose for living. I am an avid gardener. Through the years I have enjoyed the fruits of my labors in the soil. There is nothing like enjoying fresh vegetables picked right out of the garden. However, growing good fruits and vegetables is not without toil and sweat. Weeds tend to grow at a much more rapid pace and in more abundance than good vegetables.

In other words, where there is fruit growing, there are also weeds that seek to choke out and destroy it. Good habits often have corresponding opposite bad habits that consume a person whose life is void of Christ. Some of these, too numerous to list here, may be found in Romans 1:29-32, Romans 13:13, I Corinthians 5:10, II Corinthians 12:20, and I Timothy 1:9. These are listings of certain sins of the flesh that dominate a man who has not died to his own selfish nature and desires and has not allowed Christ to transform him into a fruit-producing child of God. Of course, in citing the list of nine Fruit of the Spirit in Galatians 5:22 and 23, we must also note that Paul precedes that list with another list of actions in life that are diametrically opposite to Fruit. This illuminating but non-exhaustive list (sexual immorality, impurity of mind, sensuality, worship of false gods, witchcraft, hatred, quarreling, jealousy, bad temper, rivalry, factions, party spirit, envy, drunkenness, orgies) is found in Galatians 5:19-21. All the outcroppings of "weeds" produced in one's life are what results when a person ignores Christ and decides to go his own way.

Beware of kudzu! Obviously the devil loves to produce weeds (bad habits) in our lives to keep us from God's divine purpose for our being here. A summer sight along any road in the South is kudzu sculpture. This rampant-running, green-leafed vine can cover everything it touches, and it grows so rapidly it spreads over trees, telephone poles, signs, or anything else in its path. I've never seen anything like it. For miles and miles kudzu spreads where it has not been stopped. While the intentions for bringing kudzu to our country originally were good (to stop erosion), no one could have dreamed of the widespread devastation it causes. So it is with sin. Unholy habits can totally consume a person and choke out anything fruitful or productive. Bad habits or sinful nature lingers where the Holy Spirit has not transformed a person.

Paul sums up the matter in verses 24 to 26 of that same chapter 5 in Galatians: *Those who belong to Christ have crucified their old nature with all that it loved and lusted for. If our lives are centered in the Spirit, let us be guided by the Spirit. Let us not be ambitious for our own reputations, for that only means making one another jealous* (Phillips).

CHAPTER THREE

Habit One : Learn To Love Beyond Yourself

John 13:34 – Let me give you a new command: Love one another. In the same way I loved you, you love one another. This is how everyone will recognize that you are my disciples—when they see the love you have for each other. (Msg)

LOVE – A self-sacrificing, unselfish, unconditional act of giving to the basic needs of another for that person's health, wholeness, and highest good in accordance with God's plan for his or her life.

Nate Saint, Jim Elliot, Ed McCully, Pete Fleming, and Roger Youderian were not superhuman. They were just men whose lives had been transformed by God's love. This love compelled them in 1956 to reach out to a little known tribe of cannibals in Ecuador, the Waodani, to share this love that God had put into their hearts. Even with all the signs of evil, they flew their little plane into the jungle, landed without any weapons, and stood before the Waodani to proclaim Christ. The ignorant tribesmen mistook them for gods or enemies and killed every one of them with spears. Hate was the only language they knew. But Nate, Jim, Ed, Pete, and Roger knew another language, the language of divine love. Their offering themselves as sacrifices has been an inspirational story for millions of people since Nate and Jim's wives published the book *Through Gates of Splendor* some years later.

But wait. The story doesn't end here. Nate Saint's son, Steve, has written a more recent book entitled *The End of the Spear*, which provides an update of amazing events after the massacre. The deaths of those five men opened a whole new world of understanding and compassion to the Waodani, and two years later Rachel Saint, Nate's sister, and Elizabeth Elliot, Jim's wife, demonstrated supernatural love by going themselves to live with the Waodani and transformed the lives of these natives through the power of the gospel. Rachel Saint labored to translate the New Testament into the language of the Waodani before she died in 1994. After his aunt's death, Steve Saint left a promising business career to accept an invitation from the Waodani to live among them. He and his family now live among the Waodani and are continuing to teach them the ways of God. Today Steve considers Mincaye, the native who speared and hacked his father to death with a machete, as one of his closest friends. Steve says, "These people should have been my enemies. God transformed my heart. I didn't have the formula for forgiveness. Ephesians 2:16 says Christ put enmity to death on the cross. That was something I did not fully understand in my Christian walk until I listened to God and obeyed Him and let Him write the story."[1] Now that's how love works; love is listening to God and letting Him write the story!

The essence of Christianity is *agape* love. This is what separates the Christian from the world and draws men to Christ. No love exists outside the fact that God is love. This divine attribute cannot be imitated or counterfeited. It is the most powerful force in the universe and transforms a person's entire motivation. That is why we must learn to love beyond ourselves. You can't do it alone!

Jesus embodied that love and illustrated by His life and teachings what real love is. Love never fails. It covers a multitude of sins. It is not accidental that Paul lists "love" first in his cataloging of the Fruit of the Spirit, for love truly must be present in the life of a believer before any other Fruit may be evident. Love envelops and encompasses all the other character traits Jesus demonstrated in His life; no joy, no peace, no patience, nor any other Fruit will be forthcoming without the love of God first being supernaturally imparted to a human being.

The love that Jesus displayed and taught is certainly far removed from the habits and thinking of much of the world. Witness today the strife that exists in the Middle East between races and cultures that have never understood the overpowering love of God in relationships with others. Much of the conflict in Israel, Iraq, Afghanistan, and other places is based upon habits of hate, not love. Men despise other men because of centuries of developing perspectives that are based upon hatred, jealousy, and selfish ambition. Habits of hate can be broken only by the supernatural power of God that transforms lives. That is why Christians must be the salt of the earth and live with Christlike character.

Definition of Love

Now, what is divine love exactly? **Love is a self-sacrificing, unselfish, unconditional act of giving to the basic needs of another for that person's health, wholeness, and highest good in accordance with God's plan for his or her life.**

1. First, love is an active verb. Then, as a noun, it is an **act** or choice. One writer has defined Love as "active good will."[2] Love is not a feeling or emotional outburst. Having a warm, fuzzy feeling doesn't accomplish anything. Until we have actually performed some act or made a choice to respond to someone else's need, there is not love involved, only self-gratification. Jesus repeatedly made that clear through his own acts or teachings. In fact, it was love that always made Him do what He did, even dying on the cross. Initially God so loved you and me that He gave us His only Son (John 3:16). Jesus, in turn, demonstrated that love through His own life and death.

2. Second, love is **self-sacrificing**. Before one may love, one must die to self. In John 12:24-26 Jesus used the illustration of the grain of wheat being planted and dying in order to produce much fruit: *Listen carefully: Unless a grain of wheat is buried in the ground, dead to the world, it is never any more than a grain of wheat. But if it is buried, it sprouts and reproduces itself many times over. In the same way, anyone who holds on to life just as it is destroys that life. But if you let it go, reckless in your love, you'll have it forever, real and eternal* (Msg). The secret is letting go! Regeneration, or the new birth, is the process of dying to self and being born again to the restored, fruitful life God intended for man to have on earth to begin with, and true transformation occurs when one by faith yields one's own ambitions and desires to Christ. As the Fruit of the Spirit

begins to grow in a person's life, his entire perspective and motives change. He no longer lives for self but to accomplish the will of God by being like Jesus.

3.   Third, love is **unselfish**. Selfishness is a habit that is the opposite of love. Apart from the transforming love of God, man is basically a selfish being. We learn that habit from a very early age. The self-centered, egotistical spirit of the world apart from God is so much a part of our society and thinking, it is difficult for a Christian to separate himself from that mentality until he turns to God for guidance and inspiration. Sin makes us "takers," not "givers." The selfish desire of men to take everything they can for themselves pervades our society, and accumulating "things" has become the ultimate goal of many people. Love does not respond that way. A person who has embraced Christ as Savior and Lord understands that material possessions are temporal and devotes his time and efforts to giving rather than taking.

4.   Fourth, love is **unconditional**. In other words, when a person responds in love, he does not think about getting something in return; there are no strings attached. A friend of mine has a sign on his office wall that says, "What's Your Motive?" Answering that question is the key to love. Unless love becomes a habit – a part of our very being that happens without thinking, strategizing, or manipulating – we haven't learned to love beyond ourselves. Under the anointing and guidance of the Holy Spirit, love happens daily in the life of a Christian without his trying.

5.   Then, love is **giving to the basic needs of another**. Unless giving is involved, no love has taken place. The act of love visibly occurs between individuals. In I John 3:14-15 the writer concludes, *We know that we have crossed the frontier from death to life because we do love our brothers. The man without love for his brother is living in death already. The man who actively hates his brother is a potential murderer, and you will readily see that the eternal life of God cannot live in the heart of a murderer* (Phillips). In verse 18 he sums up the situation, *My children, let us love not merely in theory or in words—let us love in sincerity and in practice* (Phillips). When God has changed a person's heart, love sees a need and responds habitually. Love happens spontaneously when a need is recognized.

A man pulls another from a burning building or life-threatening automobile accident. A woman reaches out to a friend whose life has been ravaged by cancer. A medical doctor gives up a lucrative practice and devotes his life to ministering in a third world country. In fact, Jesus said that real love occurs when we minister to those who are our enemies. Loving someone who loves me is easy. Loving beyond ourselves involves reaching out even to those who hate us.

Loving is also *forgiving*. Jesus made this point very clear in His teachings. A sure sign that love is operative in the life of a Christian is his power to forgive those who might have wronged him. Love beyond oneself does this. Nothing else could. In fact, He went even further to say that if you don't forgive, you will not be forgiven. Forgiving is the final straw test for one who claims to be truly transformed. How about that person who offended you at church? What about that dictatorial boss at work? Did you forgive the spouse who told you she didn't love you any more and left with someone else? When asked about how many times we should forgive another person, Jesus said "seventy times seven," or in other words, continuously. That's love.

6.   Love reaches out to another **for that person's health, wholeness, and highest good**. God put us here ultimately to love. Realizing that someone else is going to miss God's highest good if I don't intervene is a sobering thought. The kingdom of God is advanced because one person loves another, thus bringing a spirit of unity and harmony among people. As I love, I am influencing another person significantly through promoting his or her health and spiritual, mental, and emotional well being. As we interact with others, we represent Christ and contribute to that person's understanding of who Jesus is when we love. Peter declares, *Most of all, love each other as if your life depended on it. Love makes up for practically anything. Be quick to give a meal to the hungry, a bed to the homeless—cheerfully. Be generous with the different things God gave you, passing them around so all get in on it: if words, let it be God's words; if help, let it be God's hearty help. That way, God's bright presence will be evident in everything through Jesus, and he'll get all the credit as the One mighty in everything—encores to the end of time. Oh, yes* (I Peter 4:8-11, Msg)!

7.　Finally, our loving others is part of **God's will and plan for their lives**. God's will for my life is to affect His plan and direction for someone else's life! This interaction brings about the kingdom of God on earth and divinely draws people together. James admonishes, *My brothers, if any of you should wander away from the truth and another should turn him back on to the right path, the latter may be sure that in turning a man back from his wandering course he has rescued a soul from death, and his loving action will "cover a multitude of sins"* (James 5:19-20, Phillips). When Christians don't love, they are thwarting God's divine plan.

Several years ago someone came up with the idea of doing "random acts of kindness." Various organizations and churches have promoted this type of program of surprising a person by doing something special and out of the ordinary for him. While this exercise creates good will and calls attention to the fact that people don't often give any thought to helping others, divine love is the kind of behavior that responds daily by contributing to another person's health, wholeness, and highest good as part of God's plan for that individual's life. Christians don't have to plan to love; they just do it routinely. It becomes a habit.

Christ's Definition of Love

Now that we have defined what divine love really is, we understand that it deals with attitudes and actions. The best place to go to support this point is to listen to Jesus Himself. In the Sermon on the Mount He gives His own definition: *Ye have heard that it hath been said, Thou shalt love thy neighbor, and hate thine enemy. But I say unto you, Love your enemies, bless them that curse you, do good to them that hate you, and pray for them which despitefully use you, and persecute you* (Matthew 5:43-44, KJV). Then in John 13:34-35 He continues this thought: *Now I am giving you a new commandment – love one another. Just as I have loved you, you must love one another. This is how all men will know that you are my disciples, because you have such love for one another* (Phillips). Again, in the memorable words about the vine and the branches in John 15, He reiterates, *I have loved you just as the Father has loved me. You must go on living in my love. If you keep my commandments you will live in my love just as I have kept my Father's commandments and live in his love. I have told you this so that you can share my joy, and that your happiness may be complete. This is my commandment that you love one another as I have loved you. There is no greater love than this—that a man should lay down his life for his friends* (vs. 9-13, Phillips). Following the lines of our definition, Jesus emphasizes that love involves sharing (vs. 10) and laying down one's life for others (vs. 13).

Then He continues, *You are my friends if you do what I tell you to do. I shall not call you servants any longer, for a servant does not share his master's confidence. No, I call you friends, now, because I have told you everything that I have heard from the Father. It is not that you have chosen me; but it is I who have chosen you. I have appointed you to go and bear fruit that will be lasting; so that whatever you ask the Father in my name he will give it to you* (Phillips). The love that endures is not something we may achieve apart from Christ. It is possible only because He has chosen us and appointed us to share that love with others to help them grow (vs. 16). Only when we exercise that kind of love may we expect to ask anything in His name and have that prayer answered (vs. 16). Finally, in John 15:17 Jesus states imperatively, *This is my command: Love each other* (NIV).

Then the Apostle Paul in Philippians 2:3-5 says, *Do nothing from selfish or empty conceit, but with humility of mind let each of you regard one another as more important than himself; do not merely look out for your own personal interests but also for the interests of others. Have this attitude in yourselves which was also in Christ Jesus* (Phillips). Again in I Corinthians 16:14 he summarizes, *Let everything that you do be done in love* (Phillips). Wow! There can be no question here about motive.

A Word About Marriage

Now, if this definition of love is applicable in our relationships with others, it is doubly true with regard to one's partner for life. Claudia and I have been married now for 44 years. When we spoke our vows on August 19, 1962, we pledged ourselves to each other for life. That is the only way to go! As we have grown older together, our love for each other has matured and become more precious every day. We are one, inseparable. We'd rather do things with each other than anything else on earth. Spending time together is the most important thing for us. God has created a bond that no one can break or comprehend. True marriage is made in heaven.

Marriage between a man and woman is the nearest possible example of

God's divine love toward mankind. Perhaps the reason there are so many divorces even among Christian couples is the fact that we have forgotten what love is. In fact, marriage is the supreme test for a Christian to see if the Fruit of the Spirit is working in real life. Love, joy, peace, patience, kindness, goodness, faithfulness, gentleness, and self-control must work in tandem in a marriage for it to survive. God created marriage as a divine, eternal covenant between a man and woman, and all nine aspects of the Fruit of the Spirit are essential for true love to exist. Couples contemplating marriage would do well to examine their commitments to each other in light of the definition of love. Obviously I Corinthians 13 supports our definition and even illustrates more clearly the many dimensions of divine love. The kind of action required in true love cannot be imitated or duplicated apart from the true transformation made possible by the Holy Spirit in the life of a person completely submitted to Christ.

Sadly, it appears that the marriage ceremony in our day is more entertainment, partying, and a demonstration of all that is wrong with our culture rather than the sacred occasion for a man and woman to become one in the Spirit. Young brides- and grooms-to-be too often are more infatuated with the bachelor party, the bridesmaids' luncheon, and the wedding reception than they are intent upon making the wedding ceremony something special and divine. Some of the most raucous behavior shown on TV programs like *America's Funniest Home Videos* or *Video Bloopers* occurs at weddings, where the wedding party has deteriorated to a drunken brawl or an occasion to see how sinful we can act. How do we expect a couple to succeed in life with that kind of beginning? Engaged couples need much counseling and discussion concerning the sacredness of marriage. Then when children come along, where there is no firm biblical foundation in the home, the situation simply becomes more tragic. Holy habits must be evident in the home if they are genuine.

Love Never Fails

My friend Bill Jones was dying of kidney failure. He and his wife, Karen, had been students at Emmanuel College some years before, and we had come to admire Bill's leadership and ministry as superintendent of the Georgia Conference of the International Pentecostal Holiness Church. God was using him in a special way, but something had to be done. He had already had one transplant 19 years before, but now he was in trouble again.

The only thing keeping him alive was dialysis three times a week. This could not go on too much longer. His sister had given him a kidney before, and there was no one else in the family who was a match.

Bill and Karen prayed earnestly for an answer, and it came in a most unusual way. In Natural Bridge, Virginia, Karen had grown up with a special friend, Paula Griffin, and they had come to Emmanuel College together also. After graduating from Emmanuel, Paula and her husband, Billy, were also in ministry and learned of Bill's life-and-death situation. Without hesitating, Paula said, "I'll gladly give Bill one of my kidneys if there is a match." There was, and soon Bill and Paula were both in surgery to complete the transplant. Bill is alive and well today because of Paula's unconditional act of sacrificing herself for a friend. Now that's what love is!

Again, our definition of *love* is "a self-sacrificing, unselfish, unconditional act of giving to the basic needs of another for that person's health, wholeness, and highest good in accordance with God's plan for his or her life." To sum up our look at *agape* love, in Ephesians 5:1-2 Paul exhorts, *Live your lives in love—the same sort of love which Christ gives us and which he perfectly expressed when he gave himself up for us in sacrifice to God* (Phillips). Again, in Ephesians 4:14-15 he writes, *We are not meant to remain as children at the mercy of every chance wind of teaching and the jockeying of men who are expert in the crafty presentation of lies. But we are meant to hold firmly to the truth in love, and to grow up in every way into Christ, the head. For it is from the head that the whole body, as a harmonious structure knit together by the joints with which it is provided, grows by the proper functioning of individual parts to its full maturity in love* (Phillips). The habit of Love in the life of a Christian is essential. Its results will be life-changing.

> *Behold, the mystery of the ages has been solved.*
> *God's Love, in the form of man,*
> *Has once and for eternity paid the price.*
> *Divine Love personified came from the throne*
> *To answer once and forever man's helpless plight.*
> *Without His selfless sacrifice the world was lost,*
> *But compassion compelled Him to die,*
> *And Love raised Him from the grave!*

Lord, give me a Love that only You can inspire.
Place within my heart a supernatural fire
That will burn away all selfish pride.
Then create in me a new, compelling urge
To follow the road that Jesus trod,
A daily walk of faith to lead others to God.

CHAPTER FOUR

Habit 2: Seek Joy, Not Happiness

John 15:11 – These things have I spoken unto you, that my joy might remain in you, and that your joy might be full. (KJV)

JOY – An abiding sense of inward exultation and confidence resulting from a transformed relationship with God demonstrated through a deliberate, continuous, purposeful lifting up of the heart in thankfulness and praise to Him.

Joy and happiness are not necessarily the same. Billy Sunday said, "If you have no joy in your religion, there's a leak in your Christianity somewhere."[1] In his discussion on the Fruit of the Spirit, Mark J. Young quips, "Someone has said that joy is distinct from happiness, in that happiness depends on happenings, and if my happenings don't happen to happen the way I happen to want my happenings to happen, I'm unhappy. Joy is me being happy when my happenings don't happen to happen the way I happen to want my happenings to happen."[2] Some people think they're happy because they won the lottery, got a promotion in their work, met that special person they think will be "the one," won a football game, made a good grade in that tough course, or experienced some other temporary pleasure. All too soon, happiness fades and reality sets in. To be happy, some depend upon artificial stimuli like drugs, alcohol, sports, or pornography. Every day they try desperately to find meaning and happiness in a world of disappointment and illusion. One may be happy for a while, but circumstances can destroy that feeling quickly unless there is a firm foundation of confidence in the Word of God. Only Christ can bring true Joy.

C. S. Lewis is one of the most well known and intelligent apologists for Christianity who lived in the twentieth century. His writings emerged during the 1940s and World War II when Hitler and those who supported him were trumpeting the possibilities of an ideal world made perfect through scientific and intellectual progress. A converted atheist, Lewis began to think seriously about life and God and developed his thoughts into a number of books. His popular and inspiring work *Mere Christianity* actually began as a series of radio broadcasts on the BBC in 1941. That year he prepared a number of talks centered around "Right and Wrong" and "What Christians Believe." Other volumes followed that have endeared him to Christians of our day, and the recent commercial movie *The Chronicles of Narnia: The Lion, the Witch, and the Wardrobe*, based upon his book by that title, has given his works more visibility among 21st-century readers.

Lewis's personal testimony of his discovery of Christ is recorded in *Surprised by Joy: The Shape of My Early Life* (1955), the story of his journey from doubt to faith, from mere happiness to joy. As an intellectual, he questioned, debated, struggled, and used all the logic he could find to seek answers, and as he pointed out, "Really, a young atheist cannot guard his faith too carefully. Dangers lie in wait for him on every side."[3] His definition of Joy is not happiness but a meaningful longing for something always just out of reach. He pondered, "The very nature of joy makes nonsense of our common distinction between having and wanting."[4]

In Chapter XIV of *Surprised by Joy* he describes his exultation of discovery as a young professor at Oxford in the 1930s: "This discovery flashed a new light on my whole life. I saw that all my waitings and watchings for Joy, all my vain hopes to find some mental content on which I could, so to speak, lay my finger and say 'This is it,' had been a futile attempt to contemplate the enjoyed. ... All the value lay in that of which Joy was the desiring. And that object, quite clearly, was no state of my own mind or body at all. In a way I had proved this by elimination. I had tried everything in my own mind and body; as it were, asking myself, 'Is it this you want? Is it this?' ... I did not yet ask, Who is the desired? Only what is it? But this brought me already into the region of awe, for I thus understood that in deepest solitude there is a road right out of the self, a commerce with something which, by refusing to identify itself with any object of the senses, or anything whereof we have biological or social need, or anything imagined, or any state of our own minds, proclaims itself sheerly objective. ... And that is why we experience Joy; we yearn, rightly, for that unity which we can never reach except by ceasing to be the separate phenomenal beings called 'we.'"[5]

Surprised and convinced, C. S. Lewis discovered what every person transformed by the power of God knows. Jesus is the Joy of man's desiring. No other answer will suffice.

Definition of Joy

The Greek nouns used in the New Testament are *chara* ("joy, delight"), *agalliasis* ("exultation, exuberant joy"), and *euphrosune* ("joy, gladness").[6] Words like "joy," "joyful," and "rejoice" occur over 500 times in the Bible. Many of these references point to man's proper relationship with God. **Joy is an abiding sense of inward exultation and confidence resulting from a transformed relationship with God demonstrated through a deliberate, continuous, purposeful lifting up of the heart in thankfulness and praise to Him.**

1. **An abiding sense** – Joy is not fleeting as is happiness. The Holy Spirit puts within a person the overriding, abiding awareness that God is the blessed controller of all things regardless of circumstances, and nothing can eradicate that joy. It is the longing for things holy and righteous which creates a constant feeling of gratitude and release of worldly anxiety. Once the Christian realizes that joy is possible amid the false happiness the world provides, he develops habits of praise.

2. Joy is **an abiding sense of inward exultation and confidence**. Many times a person may try to express outward happiness by futilely attempting to demonstrate a smile or an expression of satisfaction. People strive constantly to find happiness through artificial, external means – drugs, alcohol, sex, money, material things. That kind of false happiness never satisfies. Joy is an inward exultation resulting from confident assurance which God places within the soul and spirit of a Christian.

3. Joy **results from a transformed relationship with God**. Joy must be appropriated by faith, just the same as any other divine promise. Salvation through the blood of Jesus Christ and our

confession of His Lordship brings a person into the Holy of Holies by faith and transforms a sinful, lost, unhappy soul into a jubilant son or daughter of God. This in itself ought to bring forth a habit of Joy into the life of a believer. As the songwriter described, there is "Joy unspeakable and full of glory, and the half has never yet been told."

4.   Then Joy is **demonstrated through a deliberate, continuous, purposeful lifting up of the heart**. Again, Joy is an action word. The inward exultation of limitless gratitude toward God for what He has done will habitually be demonstrated in one's countenance and behavior every day. Joy is *deliberate*; it is an act of the will. The Psalmist said, *Bless the Lord, Oh my soul, and all that is within me bless his holy name* (Psalm 103:1, KJV). We are admonished to *Make a joyful noise unto God* (Psalm 66:1, KJV). Joy is **continuous**; it does not come and go like the happiness the world offers. Paul expressed it this way: *Rejoice in the Lord always, and again I say rejoice* (Philippians 4:4, KJV). Joy is **purposeful**; there is a reason why Christians have the Joy of the Lord. They know why they're here, and they know where they're going. Joy is not dependent upon circumstances but trusts in the Lord at all times.

5.   Finally, Joy is demonstrated by **lifting up the heart in thankfulness and praise to Him**. The birth of Jesus brought angels proclaiming to the shepherds, *Fear not: for, behold, I bring you good tidings of great joy, which shall be to all people. For unto you in born this day in the City of David a Savior, which is Christ the Lord* (Luke 2:10, 11; KJV). If angels have that joy, how much more should we, who are made in God's likeness, express our thankfulness and praise to Him continually? God has promised that this Joy will not leave if we worship Him daily. In John 16:22, when Jesus is talking about His soon-coming crucifixion, He says, *And ye now therefore have sorrow: but I will see you again, and your heart shall rejoice, and your joy no man taketh from you* (KJV). What a promise that is!

Then Peter, writing in I Peter 1:7-9, expresses this ultimate Joy: *This proving of your faith is planned to bring you praise and honor and glory in the day when Jesus Christ reveals himself. And though you have never seen him, yet I know that you love him. At present you trust him without being able to see him, and even now he brings you a joy that words cannot express and which has in it a hint of the glories of heaven; and all the time you are receiving the result of your faith in him—the salvation of your own souls* (Phillips). Therefore, Joy is a by-product of our faith and trust in God's Word, our love for Him, and our hope in His soon return.

Some time ago someone sent me this little illustration by e-mail. It is tremendous:

The 92-year-old, petite, well-poised and proud lady, who is fully dressed each morning by eight o'clock, with her hair fashionably coifed and makeup perfectly applied, even though she is legally blind, moved to a nursing home today. Her husband of 70 years recently passed away, making the move necessary. After many hours of waiting patiently in the lobby of the nursing home, she smiled sweetly when told her room was ready. As she maneuvered her walker to the elevator, I provided a visual description of her tiny room, including the eyelet sheers that had been hung on her window.

"I love it," she stated with the enthusiasm of an eight-year-old having just been presented with a new puppy.

"Mrs. Jones, you haven't seen the room ... just wait."

"That doesn't have anything to do with it," she replied. "Happiness is something you decide on ahead of time. Whether I like my room or not doesn't depend upon how the furniture is arranged ... it's how I arrange my mind. I already decided to love it ... It's a decision I make every morning when I wake up. I have a choice; I can spend the day in bed recounting the difficulty I have with the parts of my body that no longer work, or get out of bed and be thankful for the ones that do. Each day is a gift, and as long as my eyes open I'll focus on the new day and all the happy memories I've stored away ... just for this time in my life."[7]

This elderly widow had discovered Joy. She understood the meaning of the verse, *The kingdom of God is not meat and drink; but righteousness, and peace, and joy in the Holy Ghost* (Romans 14:17, KJV). Like the other Fruit of the Spirit, Joy is a decision, a choice we must make daily as the Holy Spirit empowers us to give thanks and praise to our Creator and our Savior,

Jesus Christ. Joy is more than a state of mind; it is a result of an abiding confidence that God knows what is best for me and will provide the resources I need when I need them. Joy is not dependent upon current circumstances or earthly success. Rather it is the continuous inward exuberance resulting from the assurance that I am a child of God. He will never leave me or forsake me. In His presence there is *fullness of joy* (Psalm 16:11).

Other Expressions of Joy

Old and New Testament writers expressed the aspects of life that provide Joy. In Psalm 31:7 David talks about God's lovingkindness: *I will be glad and rejoice in thy mercy: for thou hast considered my trouble; thou hast known my soul in adversities* (KJV). David, the man after God's own heart who knew Joy, writes in Psalm 27:6, *And now shall mine head be lifted up above mine enemies round about me: therefore will I offer in his tabernacle sacrifices of joy; I will sing, yea, I will sing praises unto the Lord* (KJV). Again the Psalmist proclaims, *The Lord reigneth; let the earth rejoice* (Psalm 97:1, KJV).

In reference to the coming Savior, with Joy Isaiah proclaimed, *Behold, God is my salvation; I will trust and not be afraid: for the Lord JEHOVAH is my strength and my song; he also is become my salvation. Therefore with joy shall ye draw water out of the wells of salvation. And in that day shall ye say, Praise the Lord, call upon his name, declare his doings among the people, make mention that his name is exalted* (Isaiah 12:2-4, KJV). He goes on to proclaim, *And it shall be said in that day, Lo, this is our God; we have waited for him, and he will save us: this is the Lord; we have waited for him, we will be glad and rejoice in his salvation* (Isaiah 25:9, KJV). Amid Jeremiah's lament he remembered the words of God and exclaimed, *Thy words were found and I did eat them; and thy word was unto me the joy and rejoicing of mine heart: for I am called by thy name, O Lord God of Hosts* (Jeremiah 15:16, KJV). The familiar words of Nehemiah in chapter 8, verse 10, also bring encouragement: *The joy of the Lord is your strength* (KJV).

As is true with each of the Fruit of the Spirit, Joy is present as a by-product of other healthy spiritual habits. A single instrument in an orchestra sounds one dimensional, but put them all together and you have a beautiful symphony. The Christian's expressions of love, joy, peace, patience, gentleness, goodness, faithfulness, meekness, and self-control work together to produce the kind of orchestra that will be harmonious. No one knew this better than Paul, who wrote in Romans 15:13, *May the God of hope fill you with joy and peace in your faith, that by the power of the Holy Spirit, your whole life and outlook may be radiant with hope* (Phillips). And in his letter to the Christians at Colossae he admonishes, *We are asking God that you may see things, as it were, from his point of view by being given spiritual insight and understanding. We also pray that your outward lives, which men see, may bring credit to your master's name, and that you may bring joy to his heart by bearing genuine Christian fruit, and that your knowledge of God may grow yet deeper* (Colossians 1:9-10, Phillips). To the Philippians he requested, *Fulfill ye my joy, that ye be like-minded, having the same love, being of one accord, of one mind. Let nothing be done through strife or vainglory; but in lowliness of mind let each esteem other better than themselves* (2:2-3, KJV).

Even the practical James had something to say about the relationship of Joy to the victorious life of a Christian. In Chapter 1, verses 2-4, he writes, *My brethren, count it all joy when ye fall into divers temptations; Knowing this, that the trying of your faith worketh patience. But let patience have her perfect work, that ye may be perfect and entire, wanting nothing* (KJV). Joy can even be present in the direst of circumstances when we realize that God is trying to perfect us for His work.

Finally, the words of the greatest Teacher of all were replete with Joy. The word *blessed* used in the Beatitudes in Matthew 5 could easily be translated "joyful" or "happy." Joyful are the poor in spirit, joyful are they that mourn, joyful are the meek, joyful are they which hunger and thirst after righteousness, joyful are the merciful, joyful are the pure in heart, joyful are the peacemakers, and joyful are they who are persecuted for righteousness' sake. In His parables Jesus uses the word *joy* in relation to the treasure found in the field (Matthew 13:44), the increase of the talents (Matthew 25:21-23), the lost sheep (Luke 15:4-7), the lost coin (Luke 15:8-10), the prodigal son (Luke 15:24). As He illustrated in the parables, Joy is apparently not just an earthly opportunity, but the angels in heaven also rejoice when we give our lives to Christ. Then in the same chapter in John where He talks about the importance of the vine and the branches, Jesus says, *These things have I spoken unto you that my joy might remain in you, and that your joy might be full* (John 15:11, KJV). Again, the Psalmist David foresaw what Christ was to do, for he proclaimed, *Weeping may endure for a night, but joy cometh in the morning* (Psalm 30:5, KJV).

Music Is Audible Joy

Those who know me know I love to sing. I don't believe there is any better way to experience joy than through a song. Claudia and I keep our kitchen radio tuned into a Christian station that plays beautiful music all day long. Our car radio is tuned to the same station. One of the first things I do in the morning as I drink my coffee is turn on the radio and sing along with the artists. How refreshing and inspiring. A composer's joy spills out into song; it just has to! The rest of us benefit from the writer's joy by learning and repeating these words put to music.

The best songs are the ones that talk about joy. Think of the titles you love. David the shepherd boy and Psalmist sang for joy, the angels announcing the birth of Jesus shouted for joy, and gifted songwriters for centuries have written words of joy put to music. Try singing when you're down. Listen to uplifting CDs. I grew up in Memphis, Tennessee, during the heyday of gospel quartets like the Blackwood Brothers and the Statesmen, so I still have that music in me. Watching Bill Gaither's Homecoming videos is one of my favorite things to do, but I like other contemporary music as well when the words express joy.

Down through the ages man has expressed joy through his music. I have lived through a number of phases or fads in Christian music, but music of any age that glorifies God and gives praise to Him is good. I grew up singing the wonderful hymns by Fanny Crosby, Charles Wesley, Isaac Watts, and other earlier composers. Then in the 1970s scripture choruses became the rage, and we learned to sing Psalms and other key verses in the Bible as musicians followed the leading of the Spirit. I can still sing numerous scriptures and enjoy doing so. Bill Gaither came along and revived Southern gospel, and we started singing the many compositions he and Gloria wrote. More recently, contemporary gospel has taken over, and many young musicians and singers have revolutionized the music of God. Whatever the case, when a person longs to express his love for the Lord and the joy He brings, music is the answer. God knew we would have difficulty expressing Joy, so He gifted songwriters to help us. Aren't you glad?

Abiding Joy

Joy is present at the moment one is converted. Joy continues as a Christian grows in discipleship. And Joy is a product of Christian service. Have you ever known someone who rejoiced at all times, a person who never seemed to be discouraged? Illness does not destroy this eternal Joy; lack of money does not take Joy away. The absence of material things cannot take away one's Joy. Not even death can destroy Joy.

I have known a few Christians who demonstrate this Joy, and what an encouragement they have been! One of them is Nancy Beatty. Nancy just turned 70, but you would never know it. She is a retired elementary school teacher whose joy overflows wherever she goes. I've never heard Nancy speak negatively about anyone or anything. She brings joy into any situation by her smile and genuine concern for others. In spite of her aches and pains, Nancy is always ministering to and mentoring others, and her daily routine is filled with sharing her joy with anyone who will happen to come her way whether she is at Curves, the grocery store, school, or church. Nancy laughs at herself as much as anything. She never complains. It is great to see someone grow older without growing bitter. Lord, give us more Joy!

As the songwriter put it, "If you want joy, real joy, wonderful joy, let Jesus come into your heart. Your sins He'll wash away, your night He'll turn to day, your life He'll make it over anew. If you want joy, real joy, wonderful joy, let Jesus come into your heart."

Again, our definition of Joy is "an abiding sense of inward exultation and confidence resulting from a transformed relationship with God demonstrated through a deliberate, continuous, purposeful lifting up of the heart in thankfulness and praise to Him." In summary, real Joy is a Christian distinctive. No one knows the joy of forgiveness like a Christian. The Psalmist shouted, *Blessed is he whose transgression is forgiven, whose sin is covered.... Be glad in the Lord, and rejoice, ye righteous: and shout for joy, all ye that are upright in heart* (Psalm 32:1-11, KJV). No one has the joy that comes from serving others like a Christian. Paul rejoiced at what God was doing for his fellow Christians at Collossae: *For though I am a long way away from you in body, in spirit I am by your side, watching like a proud father the solid steadfastness of your faith in Christ. Just as you received Christ, so go on living in him—in simple faith. Grow out of him as a plant grows out of the soil it is planted in, becoming more and more sure of the faith as you were taught it, and your lives will overflow with joy and thankfulness* (Colossians 2:5-7, Phillips). And no one has experienced transformational joy like a Christian when he comes to know Jesus Christ as his personal Savior and Lord!

Joy gushed forth from my soul like a gigantic dam had burst,
And much to my surprise God's lavish love flooded my soaring spirit.
At that marvelous moment I knew the reason He sent His special Son
To restore in me the long lost hope and revive in me His glory!
Since that life-illuminating change has overwhelmed my soul,
I will forever lift my heart and voice in thankfulness and praise to Him!

CHAPTER FIVE

Habit 3: Follow Peace You Cannot Find Alone

Philippians 4:7 – And the peace of God, which passeth all understanding, shall keep your hearts and minds through Christ Jesus. (KJV)

PEACE – A profound, pervasive sense of continuous contentment made possible by the assurance of the Holy Spirit that Jesus is alive and God is in control of all things.

Come on. Sing it with me. You know this old hymn:
> *Far away in the depths of my spirit tonight*
Rolls a melody sweeter than psalm;
In celestial-like strains it unceasingly falls
O'er my soul like an infinite calm.
What a treasure I have in this wonderful peace,
Buried deep in the heart of my soul;
So secure that no power can mine it away
While the years of eternity roll.
Peace! Peace! Wonderful peace,
Coming down from the Father above;
Sweep over my spirit forever I pray,
In fathomless billows of love.
> (W. G. Cooper)

Now in those words W. G. Cooper captured very well the essence of God's peace that can permeate the human soul that is totally transformed by the power of the Holy Spirit. A Christian just singing those words finds a deep, settled sense of assurance in the truth they express. Only Christ can produce that kind of peace.

On the other hand, if the Fruit of Peace is not present or demonstrated in the life of a Christian on a consistent, daily basis, the world is not going to see the difference peace makes amid the struggles, turmoil, war, evil, strife, and conflict that are so much a part of our earthly existence. Reading the papers, listening to the news, or just hearing people express their fears, frustrations, and confusion is enough to cause one to despair. Our world today is certainly far from the peaceful existence God intended. Every day in Iraq, Afghanistan, Israel, Sudan, Nepal, Egypt, and countless other countries around the world, we read of bloodshed caused by hatred, anger, and lust for power. The world is hungry for peace, but it won't happen without recognizing the Prince of Peace.

Definition of Peace:
Peace is a profound, pervasive sense of continuous contentment made possible by the assurance of the Holy Spirit that Jesus is alive and God is in control of all things:

> 1. This Peace is **profound**. In other words, it is beyond our comprehension. We can't explain it; we can't fake it. This is the Peace that Horatio G. Spafford experienced even after his wife and daughters were lost at sea in a terrible storm. He wrote, *When peace, like a river, attendeth my way,/When sorrows like sea billows roll—/ Whatever my lot, Thou hast taught me to say,/It is well, it is well with my soul.*[1] Inside Horatio Spafford was the calm assurance that death was not the end and that he would see his family again someday. Peace is wellness of soul; it is unshakable and unchanging.

> 2. This Peace is **pervasive**. It is abundant and thoroughly saturates our lives when we know Christ. Nothing can shake it. Peace covers our souls like a river flooding away any sorrow or sadness the world may try to place there.

> 3. This Peace is **a sense of continuous contentment**. Down deep within our soul is the conviction that everything is all right. Furthermore, the sensitivity to the Holy Spirit keeps us constantly aware that all is well. Disappointments, diseases, financial

setbacks, uncertainties, death – none of these things will shake a truly transformed Christian's Peace. In his letter to the Christians at Philippi, Paul declared, *Don't fret or worry. Instead of worrying, pray. Let petitions and praises shape your worries into prayers, letting God know your concerns. Before you know it, a sense of God's wholeness, everything coming together for good, will come and settle you down. It's wonderful what happens when Christ displaces worry at the center of your life* (Philippians 4:6, 7, Msg). A more familiar rendering of verse 7, from the King James Version, is *And the peace of God, which passeth all understanding, shall keep your hearts and minds through Christ Jesus.* Then, in verse 11 of that same chapter Paul makes a powerful statement concerning the Peace that only comes from God: ... *I have learned, in whatever state I am, therewith to be content* (KJV). That is the Peace you cannot find alone!

4.   This Peace is **made possible by the assurance of the Holy Spirit**. We are born to worry; babies start out fretting. Then that sense of despair and inability to cope just gets worse the older we get. There is a battle raging within the souls of men when God's deep, settled Peace is absent. No wonder people in our day cannot find contentment and satisfaction in life. They are desperately searching for Peace in the midst of the storms of a world without meaning apart from the transformation that comes with commitment to Jesus Christ. Only the power of the grace of God through the Holy Spirit's tugging at your heart can bring the calm assurance that all is well.

5.   Peace knows **that Jesus is alive**. He is the *Prince of Peace* (Isaiah 9:6). His coming removed the enmity between God and man and reconciled sinful man to God the Father. When He was born, the angels proclaimed, *Glory to God in the highest, and on earth peace, good will toward men* (Luke 2:14, KJV). Before He left his human form, he declared, *I leave behind with you—peace; I give you my own peace and my gift is nothing like the peace of this world. You must not be distressed and you must not be daunted* (John 14:27, Phillips). Paul the Apostle reiterated, *Since it is by faith that we are justified, let us grasp the fact that we have peace with God through our Lord Jesus Christ. Through him we have confidently entered into this new relationship of grace, and here we take our stand, in happy*

certainty of the glorious things he has for us in the future (Romans 5:1-2, Phillips). Paul reinforces this miraculous transformation in Ephesians 2 when he says, *You were without Christ; you were utter strangers to God's chosen community, the Jews; and you had no knowledge of, or right to, the promised agreements. You had nothing to look forward to and no God to whom you could turn. But now, through the blood of Christ, you who were once outside the pale are with us inside the circle of God's love and purpose. For Christ is our living peace. He has made a unity of the conflicting elements of Jew and Gentile by breaking down the barrier which lay between us. By his sacrifice he removed the hostility of the Law, with all its commandments and rules, and made himself out of the two, Jew and Gentile, one new man, thus producing peace* (Ephesians 2:12-15, Phillips). Praise God, He is our Peace. He has broken down every wall of hate, evil, and enmity!

6.   Then Peace is the awareness that **God is in control of all things**. Regardless of how bleak and barren the picture appears to be, the Peace of God tells a truly transformed Christian that He is in control. He knows what is best. Many of the present anxieties, preoccupation with things that are not really that earth-shaking, fade away when God's Peace pervades our lives. Life is filled with uncertainties, disappointments, and worries when we focus on our weaknesses, but when we look to Jesus, He gives the confidence that is needed to keep this Peace of mind, heart, and spirit. Paul proclaimed, *Delight yourselves in God; yes, find your joy in him at all times. Have a reputation for gentleness, and never forget the nearness of your Lord. Don't worry over anything whatever; tell God every detail of your needs in earnest and thankful prayer, and the peace of God, which transcends human understanding, will keep constant guard over your hearts and minds as they rest in Christ Jesus* (Philippians 4:4-7, Phillips).

A Personal Testimony

I know firsthand about this Peace. Some years ago in December (35 to be exact) when our son, Mark, was about three years old, he became very tired and listless and continued to run a high fever even after taking antibiotics. Our local physician examined him a second time and noticed that he had difficulty raising his head. He then recommended that we take him to a pediatrician for further testing. We made an appointment with a wonderful Asian pediatrician, a dedicated lady who had cared for many children through the years. She examined him, noticed his fatigue and inability to walk very well, and decided that he needed to have fluid drawn from his spine for some tests.

We waited all day in his hospital room for her report, and finally she came that evening with a sad look on her face. She said, "I had to go home and lie down awhile before coming to tell you this. I really regret to have to tell you the tests show that Mark has meningitis. We need to transfer him to the Children's Hospital at Emory so that they may treat him more completely." Needless to say, our Peace was shattered. We had never gone through anything like this in our lives. Here it was Christmas time. We were healthy, our children were healthy, and everything seemed to be going well. I had left a good teaching position in a public school system and community college to answer the call to Christian higher education at a small college without the same benefits and salary available before, so naturally we were fearful and troubled by the prospects of Mark's condition. Worried and anxious, we asked ourselves the same question most people ask in this kind of situation, "Why, Lord? Why is this happening to us? We have tried to be faithful and have sacrificed much for You. We don't understand."

We spent a sleepless night with my parents, who were living in Athens, Georgia, at the time, where my dad was a pastor. The hospital was about 30 miles from our house, so I got up the next morning and drove home to pack some of Mark's things to take to the hospital in Atlanta. I have never experienced the depth of despair of that 30-mile drive. Amid my self-pity and lack of faith I certainly did not have Peace. We had never been tested like this.

As everyone knows, meningitis is a dreaded disease with all kinds of possible physical and mental damage to the person. We had seen and known others whose lives were shattered by this horrible, crippling disease, and the devil brought all this to my mind as I drove. Claudia and I had wept until we could cry no more. The situation looked hopeless.

I walked into the empty house and viewed the Christmas decorations my wife had labored so long to put up and the presents under the Christmas tree. Then I walked into Mark's bedroom. At that point I looked around his room at his toys, clothes, and personal items and lost control. With a heart heavier than a ten-ton truck I cried, "Lord, I don't understand why this is happening. We have cried, prayed, and reasoned all we know to do, and I don't know why this has happened. But you are Lord; you gave him to us, and we dedicated him to you when he was born. He is yours. We give him back to you. If you see fit to take him now, we accept that as your will. We will not fight any longer."

I cannot adequately describe to you what happened at that moment. All of a sudden I felt a Peace wash over my spirit that I had never known. Christ was in that room with me and spoke to me as clearly as I have ever heard anyone audibly. He said, "That is what I have been waiting to hear. Rest in my promises and do not be afraid. All is well."

Immediately I knew Mark was going to be all right. That assurance did not leave me. I gathered up some of his clothes and jubilantly headed back to the hospital. By the time I walked into his room Mark was sitting up in bed eating a cheese toast (his favorite) and smiling. His fever was gone, his strength had returned, and when the doctor examined him, she was shocked to find him completely healed! As we took Mark home on Christmas Day, it was the most wonderful, meaningful Christmas we have ever celebrated. We learned a valuable lesson through that experience, and that Peace we could not find alone has never left us to this day. We've been through other trials and tests, but the memory of that day will bring comfort and contentment for the rest of our lives.

Oh, and by the way, Mark was not physically or mentally affected by the meningitis. He went on to graduate with honors from high school and was valedictorian of his college graduating class. He and his wife, Amy, are pastoring in Virginia and have three children.

Obstacles to Peace

Now we have looked at the definition of Peace, let's consider some of the obstacles that Satan puts in our way. As we have already noted, anxiety and worry about insignificant and uncontrollable things may destroy Peace. Then strife, jealousy, and envy all work to inhibit the Holy Spirit's power in our lives to produce the Fruit of Peace. Through our own misgivings and lack of perception of God's will, we may unconsciously contribute not only to our own problems, but because of jealousy or envy bring strife to someone else's life.

There are so many questions we cannot answer that are in God's hands, it is detrimental to dwell on them. Even indifference and apathy can also create an unhealthy disregard for God's deity and power to transform our thinking and behavior. Peace is not enhanced by lack of concern or involvement. Spiritual carelessness often leads to defeat in the life of a Christian, and apathy may bring conflict.

Be a Peacemaker

Jesus said, *Blessed are the peacemakers, for they will be called the children of God* (Matthew 5:9 KJV). When the Fruit of Peace is operating in the life of a Christian, he develops the habit of mediation and resolution of conflict regardless of the circumstances. This inner Peace Paul describes in Romans 5:1: *Therefore being justified by faith we have peace with God through our Lord Jesus Christ* (KJV). Before one may become a peacemaker, he must be at peace with himself. As Paul points out, this is possible only because of our reconciliation to God made possible by the death and resurrection of Jesus. We are made new creations when we come to the foot of the cross of Christ and confess our inability to have true Peace apart from Him. Only when we have yielded to the gentle wooing of the Holy Spirit and confessed our sins may we truly have Peace. Genuine transformation takes place when we recognize that we are justified by faith in Jesus Christ alone. From that point Peace prevails.

When the Fruit of Peace is present in the life of a believer, he or she becomes a catalyst for the kingdom of God. This Peace produces harmony and unity in the Body of Christ. In Ephesians 4:1-3 Paul cautions, *I therefore, the prisoner of the Lord, beseech you that ye walk worthy of the vocation wherewith ye are called. With all lowliness and meekness, with longsuffering, forbearing one another in love; Endeavoring to keep the unity of the Spirit in the bond of peace* (KJV). As the Lord builds His church, He is depending upon peacemakers to stand as sentries of the peace among the family. In that enlightening third chapter of Colossians where Paul is specifying sinful habits to shun, he also enumerates habits to "put on," a listing similar to the Fruit he outlines in Galatians 5:22 and 23. In addition to mentioning kindness, humility, meekness, longsuffering, forbearance, forgiveness, and love, he says, *And let the peace of God rule in your hearts, to the which also ye are called in one body: and be ye thankful* (Colossians 3:15, KJV). Too often in situations of debate among members of the church, the Fruit of Peace is not evident. Rather, the devil has a thrill as Christians divide and fight among themselves, often resulting in church splits and bitter rivalry.

The presence of Peace will prevent division.

The Perfect Peacemaker

The role of the peacemaker is clearly described by Jesus in the Sermon on the Mount. He revolutionizes the concept of love and peace as He says, *You have heard that it used to be said "Thou shalt love thy neighbor and hate thy enemy," but I tell you, Love your enemies, and pray for those who persecute you, so that you may be sons of your Heavenly Father* (Matthew 5:43-45, Phillips). We are to love even our enemies and pray for those who oppose us or create situations of conflict. This procedure should be a habit.

Then the well known instructions of Jesus in Matthew 15 help to further the cause of peace: *If a fellow believer hurts you, go and tell him – work it out between the two of you. If he listens, you've made a friend. If he won't listen, take one or two others along so that the presence of witnesses will keep things honest, and try again. If he still won't listen, tell the church. If he won't listen to the church, you'll have to start over from scratch, confront him with the need for repentance, and offer again God's forgiving love. Take this most seriously: A yes on earth is yes in heaven; a no on earth is no in heaven. What you say to one another is eternal. I mean this. When two of you get together on anything at all on earth and make a prayer of it, my Father in heaven goes into action. And when two or three of you are together because of me, you can be sure that I'll be there* (Matthew 18:15-20, Msg). A peacemaker is in the habit of being open and honest with others, even those who may be contentious or who have sinned. Instead of spreading gossip and idle talk about the person who has a problem or conflict with you, go to him or her with a humble spirit and try to work things out. If more Christians would practice the habit of peaceful confrontation and loving concern, the Church would really be the instrument Christ meant it to be.

Remember? We said that the Fruit of the Spirit work together simultaneously to produce healthy spiritual habits. Peace results when Joy abounds and Love is unconditional. Paul says, *Even if a man should be detected in some sin, my brothers, the spiritual ones among you should quietly set him back on the right path, not with any feeling of superiority but being yourselves on guard against temptation. Carry one another's burdens and so live out the law of Christ* (Galatians 6:1-2, Phillips).

While history has recorded civilization after civilization that has risen and fallen because of hatred, strife, war, and selfishness, one cannot help but wonder if results might have been different if men had heeded the words of Jesus and followed peace first. Even Christian nations have lived and died by the sword instead of turning to peaceful attempts to resolve conflict. In the Middle Ages the Church evidently forgot the Fruit of the Spirit and lived by power, control, and strategy. However, don't give up hope. We in this 21st century can make a difference through habits of Peace. Personal peace with God produces peace among our neighbors and nations. The problem is that men strive in vain to find peace by themselves or to coerce others to follow their idea of peace. Paul's admonition to the Roman Christians was *May the God of hope fill you with joy and peace in your faith, that by the power of the Holy Spirit, your whole life and outlook may be radiant with hope* (Romans 15:13, Phillips). Peace on earth will never happen without the presence of the Prince of Peace!

Again, our definition of Peace is "a profound, pervasive sense of continuous contentment made possible by the assurance of the Holy Spirit that Jesus is alive and God is in control of all things." Peace is possible only by practicing the presence of God. As we focus our faith upon Him, study to show ourselves worthy, pray without ceasing, and love His Word, the habit of knowing Peace will pervade our spirit. Peter wrote, *He that would love life, And see good days, Let him refrain his tongue from evil, And his lips that they speak no guile: And let him turn away from evil, and do good; Let him seek peace and pursue it* (I Peter 3:10-11, Phillips).

Finally, of Peace James declares, *The wisdom that comes from God is first utterly pure, then peace-loving, gentle, approachable, full of tolerant thoughts and kindly actions, with no breath of favoritism or hint of hypocrisy. And the wise are peacemakers who go on quietly sowing for a harvest of righteousness—in other people and in themselves* (James 3:17-18, Phillips). There, my friend, is the key to Peace you will never find alone.

> *Perfect, profound Peace is possible in a world of war*
> *Where swirling storms stir the souls of men*
> *And horrendous hate keeps nations apart.*
> *Amid the strife, the turmoil, and the care*
> *The Holy Spirit broods and breathes*
> *Everlasting life to calm our finite fears.*
> *He saturates our souls with the assurance*
> *That all is well and God is in control!*

CHAPTER SIX

Habit 4: Extablish A Pattern Of Patience

I Corinthians 13:4 – *The love of which I speak is slow to lose patience – it looks for a way of being constructive.* (Phillips)

PATIENCE (LONGSUFFERING) – A certainty of God's unfailing faithfulness to His promises amid perplexing circumstances that results in a steadfastness in obedience despite time limitations or pressure to deny Him.

Talking to other vehicles while driving runs in my family. I guess my children took after me in this regard. If I happen to get behind a slow-moving pick-up truck on a two-lane stretch where passing is impossible, I start talking to the driver under my breath, making comments like, "Please go on. Why can't you see that there is a line of cars behind you trying to get somewhere. What's wrong with you? Did you decide to take your truck out for a walk or what?" Another annoying situation occurs on the interstate when a car or truck gets in the left-hand lane and goes too slowly to pass the vehicle in the right-hand lane, holding up traffic behind him. My usual comment is "Go on! Can't you see you're keeping all these cars from getting by?" I've discovered that my son and daughter do the same thing. I get amused at their comments when riding with them. My son, Mark, has always been a good dramatist. In college he was involved in a theater group, and he has a tremendous gift of acting out situations in his sermons that captivate an audience. And, boy, does he become animated when someone cuts in front of him in traffic or runs a red light at the crossing he has entered. "What is wrong with that woman?" "Did you see what that man just did?" Now don't laugh too much. You know you do the same thing. Impatience is a part of life in the fast lane.

In this hurry-up microsecond world of today one of the most difficult holy habits for us to establish is patience or longsuffering. In a society of digital cameras, instant photos, fast food, rapid access Internet, online shopping, satellite TV, advanced computer technology, space exploration, scanned credit card purchases, interstate highways, and jet travel, patience is hard to find. Overworked and overstressed businessmen and -women spend hours on the freeway fighting rush-hour traffic to get to pressure-packed jobs difficult to maintain and have precious little time to relax and let God speak. For a truly transformed Christian to be able to establish a pattern of patience, surely the Holy Spirit must intervene. Nothing short of the miracle-working power of God can produce patience in a person's life. But it is possible!

Noah obeyed God when no one else cared or believed and for many years patiently built the ark. Abraham proved to be longsuffering as God moved him to a far country about which he knew nothing. He walked step by step with God, allowing Yahweh to give the order for next move. Job lost everything he possessed but never gave up hope that his Redeemer lived. Sold into slavery and far from family and home, for years Joseph patiently waited for God to deliver him from Potiphar's wife and prison to a place of prominence and power. Moses wandered in the wilderness for 40 years as God shaped his preparation for leading the people of Israel out of Egypt. In his relationship to King Saul, David certainly demonstrated longsuffering, enduring many attempts at his life even after he had been anointed king in Saul's place. After his dramatic conversion on the road to Damascus, Paul patiently waited for three years in the desert before God launched the greatest missionary career of all time. John lingered alone of the Isle of Patmos until the Holy Spirit revealed to him the mysteries of the book of Revelation.

Definition of Patience

Now let's consider the definition of the Fruit of Patience or Longsuffering: **Patience is a certainty of God's unfailing faithfulness to His promises**

amid perplexing circumstances that results in a steadfastness in obedience despite time limitations or pressure to deny Him.

1.   Patience is synonymous with **certainty**. For patience to be present in the life of a Christian, there must be a certainty of God's overall control of everything that happens. Throughout all his suffering, Paul confidently proclaimed, *I have become absolutely convinced that neither death nor life, neither messenger of Heaven nor monarch of earth, neither what happens today nor what may happen tomorrow, neither a power from on high nor a power from below, nor anything else in God's whole world has any power to separate us from the love of God in Jesus Christ our Lord* (Romans 8:38, 39; Phillips).

2.   Patience presupposes **God's unfailing faithfulness to His promises**. A steadfast faith in our Creator produces patience. His promises and love are unwavering; He never changes His mind or word. God is aware of all situations and is totally loyal and true. He has promised never to leave us, even to the end of the age. Impatience in a perplexing situation denies that God is faithful to his promises and demonstrates a lack of trust in His sovereignty. In the early 19th century a man named William Carey answered the call to reach the people of India with the gospel. These were difficult times, and few men would have moved with a sick wife to Serampore, India, to attempt to translate the Bible into multiple Indian languages. While Carey was away on a teaching trip, his print shop caught on fire and burned to the ground. In addition to many of his valuable books, lost were sets of type for 14 eastern languages, 1,200 reams of paper, 55,000 printed sheets, and 30 pages of his Bengal dictionary. Instead of giving up he wrote, "We are not discouraged; indeed the work is already begun again in every language. We are cast down but not in despair."[1] On another occasion he penned, "There are grave difficulties on every hand, and more are looming ahead. Therefore we must go forward."[2]

3.   Patience endures **amid perplexing circumstances**. There are actually two words in the Greek that refer to patience. The first, *makrothumia,* is used with reference to patience with persons; the second, *hupomonaa,* with things or circumstances.[3] W. E. Vine says, "Longsuffering is that quality of self-restraint in the face of

provocation which does not hastily retaliate or promptly punish. It is the opposite of anger and is associated with mercy, and is used of God."[4] In other words, sometimes we become impatient or intolerant when it comes to relationships with other people, and at other times we fail to exercise patience when we face unforeseen or extreme trials and testings. How quickly Christians join into the criticism and condemnation when a fellow follower of Christ fails or goes astray! At other times we fail to understand why suffering or pain comes into our lives and blame God for the situation. Abraham and Sarah couldn't wait for God to carry out His promise for an heir, so they took matters into their own hands. Thus Ishmael was born of Sarah's handmaiden, Hagar, and hostility has existed in the Middle East to this day. After God's miraculous delivery of the Israelites from Pharaoh's Egyptian bondage, they often became impatient with Moses, constantly complaining about something affecting their convenience or comfort. King Saul became impatient when the Priest Samuel failed to arrive to perform the sacrifice as God required and did it himself. His life was never the same again. Impetuous Peter constantly got himself into difficulty by his lack of patience, ultimately denying his dying Lord three times. Through the inspiration of the Holy Spirit a truly transformed Christian patiently waits for God's next move and does not become anxious when circumstances are perplexing.

4.   Patience **results in a steadfastness in obedience**. Here the operative word is *obedience*. Bill Gothard's definition of obedience is "Freedom to be creative under the protection of divinely appointed authority."[5] Obedience is tough when things aren't going my way, but the test of time is critical in the life of a truly transformed Christian. Patience must involve obedience to the limitations life places upon us through God's eternal laws.

5.   Patience remains steadfast **despite time limitations or pressure to deny Him**. Sometimes staying put because God says to is the most difficult thing to do. Longsuffering is just what the word implies. One may have to suffer for a long period before seeing the divine meaning of the events unfolding in one's life. Instead of trusting God in a crisis, we leave Him entirely out of our thinking. Too many times we become restless and anxious about

God's timetable, failing to see beyond our own loss, inconvenience, or interruption. In reality impatience is a practical atheism, a denial of God's sovereignty. Again, Bill Gothard defines Patience as "Accepting a difficult situation from God without giving Him a deadline to remove it."[6] In his book *Fruits and Gifts of the Spirit*, Father Thomas Keating says, "Long-suffering is certitude in God's unwavering fidelity to his promises. Our security is no longer based on anything we might possess or accomplish, but rather on our conviction of God's unfailing protection and readiness to forgive. Hence we are not easily disturbed by the ebb and flow of human events and our emotional reactions to them. Feelings continue to be felt, at times more strongly than ever, but they no longer dominate our awareness or our activity. We are content to wait with confidence for God's deliverance in every situation, especially during prolonged periods of dryness and the dark nights."[7]

A Trial of Patience

In 1990 my wife and I, along with all the Emmanuel College family, were ecstatic about the fact that God had opened the door for the College to expand its academic programs to add a number of four-year liberal arts majors. Until that time Emmanuel had offered only freshman and sophomore courses in General Education, allowing a majority of students to transfer their credits to another four-year college or university. The only four-year degree offered was the Bachelor of Science or Bachelor of Arts degree in Religion, a program that had been in operation since 1973. The International Pentecostal Holiness Church, the College's sponsoring denomination, had overwhelmingly expressed a desire to see Emmanuel become a four-year, liberal arts institution to serve more effectively the youth of the Church and surrounding community. The long, involved process of applying for and receiving regional accreditation for the four-year majors was complete, and Emmanuel was on the brink of making history. That's when it happened.

First, I discovered I had an intestinal problem when I began to bleed internally. The gastroenterologist's first diagnosis was intestinal cancer, but after he scared us half to death, the test came back negative. I stayed in the hospital for several days debating about having surgery but elected to go with treatment by prednisone to see if that would help heal the inflammation in my small intestine. I began to feel better and forgot about the problem for a while.

Shortly after that scary ordeal, during a routine check-up with her doctor, my wife received some very disturbing news. X-rays showed that she had a large, grapefruit-sized tumor on her ovary that had to be removed. As we tried to cope with this new development, her doctor recommended that we go to see an ovarian cancer specialist in Atlanta named Dr. Allen Lawhead. He proved to be an answer to prayer, a very compassionate, Christian surgeon. Dr. Lawhead set up a time immediately for her surgery at Georgia Baptist Hospital. We grew very anxious and impatient during this perplexing time in our lives. Both of us had been healthy all our lives and had never had to experience anything like what was happening. The timing couldn't have been worse either, with my added responsibilities at the College and the new programs just getting underway.

Suddenly our priorities shifted. We didn't know how bad Claudia's condition was and had to rely upon the Lord more than ever. The Bible became much more real to us as we searched the scriptures for answers. Psalm 91 was especially comforting, and we both memorized the entire chapter and kept repeating it for inspiration. I shall never forget Dr. Lawhead's words following the surgery, "We removed the tumor successfully. There were cancer cells present, and we can't be sure if we got them all. Your wife will need to have chemotherapy treatments for the next six months to further guard against a recurrence of the cancer." It was very clear that our patience was being tested severely. God's words in Psalm 91 came to us. We substituted Claudia's name in verses 14-16: *Because Claudia hath set her love upon me, therefore will I deliver her: I will set her on high, because she hath known my name. Claudia shall call upon me, and I will answer her: I will be with her in trouble; I will deliver her, and honour her. With long life will I satisfy Claudia, and show her my salvation"* (KJV).

The frequent trips to Atlanta for chemotherapy treatment left Claudia extremely weak and frail. I wondered if she would ever recover from the cancer. She hardly had time to recover any strength after a treatment before the next one came and zapped every ounce of energy she had. There were days when she could not even lift her head. We just kept quoting, *I will say of the Lord, He is my refuge and my fortress: my God; in him will I trust. Surely he shall deliver thee from the snare of the fowler, and from the noisome pestilence. He shall cover thee with his feathers, and under his wings shalt thou trust: his truth shall be thy shield and buckler* (Psalm 91:2-

4, KJV). Longsuffering is not easy. Patience is painful.

Finally, after six months the treatments were over, and Claudia began to claim her healing. Her strength returned gradually, and we thanked God for helping us through the long, hard days of recuperation for her. And then the enemy struck again!

One weekend in July of 1990 I began to bleed internally again, this time more severely than before. I tried to tough it out until Monday when I could see my doctor, but on Sunday evening I had lost so much blood I collapsed in the shower and had to be rushed to the hospital. The longsuffering was beginning to get longer.

On Monday Dr. Ram Reddy, my local physician, visited me in Cobb Memorial Hospital in Royston. Because of the recurrence and the severity of the situation, he recommended that I go immediately to Emory University Hospital in Atlanta for special testing and treatment. The next day I found myself in a room in Emory Hospital. That entire week gastroenterologists and interns tried every test imaginable to find out what was going on in my system. I did not eat anything the entire time. Finally, one new test they performed (while I was awake, too) revealed that a particular area of my small intestine was infected and had to be removed right away.

Now it was my turn for surgery. God again had been with us, for Dr. Lawhead, who had performed Claudia's surgery, recommended a splendid surgeon at Emory named Dr. Mike Koretz, a devout Jewish doctor who has since returned to Israel to work in a hospital there. I remember thinking before the surgery, "This is the end of my career. I will never be able to overcome this." At that time, as they wheeled me into the operating room, the words of Psalm 91 flashed into my memory, *He that dwelleth in the secret place of the most high shall abide under the shadow of the Almighty. ... Because thou hast made the Lord, which is my refuge, even the most High, thy habitation; There shall no evil befall thee, neither shall any plague come nigh thy dwelling. For he shall give his angels charge over thee, to keep thee in all his ways* (Psalm 91:1, 9-11; KJV). Dr. Koretz removed about 12 inches of my small intestine and a small part of my large intestine, including the appendix. The diagnosis was Crohn's Disease, a very rare but puzzling disorder of the intestines. A week later, when I finally arrived at home, I had lost about 25 pounds and was so weak I felt like I would never regain my stamina. All the while I felt helpless knowing that I was needed at the College to begin a new year with new momentum from the added curricula.

That was a special time for Claudia and me, as we learned the meaning of patience. Gradually we both regained our strength, God ministered mightily at the College, and we discovered His faithfulness and love in a new fresh awakening.

Sixteen years have passed. We are both still free from cancer and Crohn's Disease. God taught us some important lessons during those long, painful days of questioning and praying for His guidance. Longsuffering is learning to lean upon Him instead of your own strength; patience is trusting in His Word and listening to His voice of assurance and hope.

Once again, "Patience is a certainty of God's unfailing faithfulness to His promises amid perplexing circumstances that results in a steadfastness in obedience despite time limitations or pressure to deny Him."

> *Lord, build in me a pattern of patience,*
> *An unwavering confidence at all times*
> *Regardless of adversity and trials.*
> *Establish in me a steadfast assurance*
> *That you are working always*
> *And in every circumstance*
> *To make my life a daily diadem*
> *Of your unfailing, forever-faithful love.*

CHAPTER SEVEN

Habit 5: Keep Kindness Clearly In Focus

James 3:17 – *The wisdom that comes from God is first utterly pure, then peace-loving, gentle, approachable, full of tolerant thoughts and kindly actions, with no breath of favoritism or hint of hypocrisy.* (Phillips)

KINDNESS – An unselfish expression of compassionate concern and care whenever someone is in need physically, spiritually, or emotionally.

I have in my possession a number of two-dollar bills. I am not the only one, either. Quite a few faculty and staff members at Emmanuel College also have at least one or two. You see, on a number of occasions over the years I have received a kind note of encouragement or thanks from Dr. Ken Peden, a member of the College's School of Education until his untimely death a couple of years ago. He was habitually and constantly doing something kind for others, and along with the note was always a two-dollar bill. Even in his last stages of cancer Dr. Peden never complained but continued his acts of kindness. While his physical body continued to deteriorate over several years, if you asked him how he was doing he would simply smile and say, "Wonderful; God is good and I am blessed!" What an inspiration he was to many colleagues and students! I have not known a kinder man, and he certainly demonstrated the habit of Kindness, as well as other Fruit of the Spirit. Even after he is physically gone, I still look at those two-dollar bills and am reminded of the significance of showing kindness to others. It is a habit worth pursuing.

You see, Dr. Ken Peden had developed the healthy, holy habit of being kind to others. He had learned that God is perfectly kind and that Jesus was kindness personified. The God-type of kindness is illustrated well in the relationship between David and Jonathan, one of my favorite stories from the Old Testament. As King Saul steadily declined toward disobedience and insanity, he became more and more jealous of the young hero of Israel, David, the son of Jesse. However, Saul's son, Jonathan, became one of David's best friends, and they made a life-long covenant to help each other. David knew that Saul was trying to kill him and turned to Jonathan for support to determine the true intentions of the King. David said to Jonathan, *As for you, show kindness to your servant, for you have brought him into a covenant with you before the Lord* (I Samuel 20:8, NIV). Jonathan responded, *May the Lord be with you as he has been with my father. But show me unfailing kindness like that of the Lord as long as I live, so that I may not be killed, and do not ever cut off your kindness from my family—not even when the Lord has cut off every one of David's enemies from the face of the earth* (I Samuel 20:13-15, NIV). Years later, after Saul and Jonathan had both been killed in battle, King David remembered his promise to Jonathan and brought Jonathan's lame son, Mephibosheth, to live with him in the palace. As a trembling Mephibosheth was brought before the king, David said to him, *Don't be afraid, for I will surely show you kindness for the sake of your father Jonathan. I will restore to you all the land that belonged to your grandfather Saul, and you will always eat at my table* (II Samuel 9:7, NIV). What a great example of true, transforming Kindness that comes from an intimate relationship with God.

In his Psalms David also focused upon the kindness (translated in some cases as "goodness") of God. Hear him speak from his heart: *O taste and see that the Lord is good: blessed is the man that trusteth in him* (Psalm 34:8, KJV); *Praise ye the Lord. O give thanks to the Lord; for he is good: for his mercy endureth for ever* (Psalm 106:1, KJV); and *The Lord is good to all: and his tender mercies are over all his works* (Psalm 145:9, KJV). Then Nahum echoes these thoughts as he writes, *The Lord is good, a strong hold in the day of trouble; and he knoweth them that trust in him* (Nahum 1:7, KJV). In these verses notice that Kindness is closely akin to mercy, a comparison that is altogether fitting.

In the New Testament the use of "good" and "kind" synonymously continues. In His Sermon on the Mount Jesus pointed out, *But love ye your enemies, and do good, and lend, hoping for nothing again; and your reward shall be great, and ye shall be the children of the Highest: for he is kind unto the unthankful and to the evil* (Luke 6:35, KJV). Paul's advice to the Ephesians was *And be ye kind one to another, tenderhearted, forgiving one another, even as God for Christ's sake hath forgiven you* (Ephesians 4:32), and to the Colossians he admonished, *As, therefore, God's picked representatives of the new humanity, purified and beloved of God himself, be merciful in action, kindly in heart, humble in mind. Accept life, and be most patient and tolerant with one another, always ready to forgive if you have a difference with anyone* (Colossians 3:12, 13, Phillips). I repeat. Neither Kindness nor any other Fruit of the Spirit is possible apart from the others, and none are possible without the transforming power of the Holy Spirit operating in one's total being. In that same passage of Colossians, Paul mentions Love, Peace, Patience, and Goodness all operating along with Kindness in the life of a truly transformed person. Kindness is habit-forming if all the other Fruit are also evident in your behavior.

In all my years of working with teachers, parents, Board of Trustees' members, students, and alumni, I have known some very competent, qualified people who meant well, but Kindness was lacking in their lives. Kindness involves respect, courtesy, and consideration of others. I remember hearing a very prominent Christian medical doctor who was speaking for a faculty retreat say, "Never forget that your interruptions are your opportunities." How true that statement is, especially when our lives involve daily interaction with others! Conducting business, teaching classes, or staying with the program is important, but much more significant is our kind response to someone whose need may interrupt our routine. Kindness is a critical Fruit.

Definition of Kindness

Now let's look at our definition: **Kindness is an unselfish expression of compassionate concern and care whenever someone is in need physically, spiritually, or emotionally.**

    1.   First, Kindness is an **expression of concern and care**. Here the noun is "expression" or a visible action on the part of one person toward another. For the habit of Kindness to be operable, there must

be some action. The popular public focus by some organizations and churches called "random acts of kindness" illustrates what we are emphasizing. Kindness is demonstrated in some tangible behavior, just as Love is. In fact, Kindness is inseparably connected to Love, as are all of the other eight Fruit of the Spirit. Synonyms for Kindness would include words like *availability, usefulness,* and *gentleness.* The Greek word is *chrestotes,* meaning "serviceable, good, pleasant."[1] Some translations of Galatians 5:22 and 23 (such as the KJV) actually use Gentleness instead of Kindness in the list of Fruit. Another Greek word used in some instances is *philanthropia,* meaning charitable beneficence, from which we get our word *philanthropy.*[2] Other more modern translations use Kindness. Actually Gentleness is Kindness in the very best and most complete definition of the term. In his letter to the Christians at Thessalonica, Paul wrote, *We were gentle among you, even as a nurse cherisheth her children* (I Thess. 2:7, KJV). His illustration here is comparing the care a nurse (or a mother) has for a sick or needy child to the gentleness one Christian should have for another hurting person. The truly transformed Christian recognizes that there are many "sick" brothers and sisters who exhibit the same characteristics as the physically ill child – loss of (spiritual) appetite, irritability, anger, a dislike for work, aloofness, etc. Bill Gothard's definition of Gentleness is "showing personal care and concern in meeting the need of others."[3]

2.   Kindness (or Gentleness) is an **unselfish** expression of concern. Again, the adjective "unselfish" is the same word we used in our definition of Love. Kindness is visible Love. Then Kindness is directly opposite to selfishness or pride. One who is self-centered or proud is obviously not interested in someone else's need. The habit of Kindness, divinely implanted into the heart of a truly transformed Christian, is cultivated every day in relationships – at home, at work, at school, or wherever one's daily activities take him.

3.   Next, Kindness is an expression of **compassionate concern and care**. Compassion may be defined as sorrow for the suffering of another, pity, or deep sympathy. Kindness, then, is the tangible evidence of that feeling, which translates into some action on behalf of the person less fortunate. The opposite reaction would be harshness or carelessness. Even after all of God's dealing with Jonah

to get him to preach to the pagan people of Nineveh, he still showed little sympathy or compassion for them, thinking only of his own misery and suffering. God had to use a gourd and a worm to teach Jonah a lesson on Kindness and compassion (Jonah 4:2-11). Treating another person, Christian or non-Christian, harshly or carelessly is far removed from the character of Christ, who, for example, had compassion on the Samaritan woman drawing water from the well, for Zaccheus, the little rich publican everyone despised, the widow from Nain whose son had died, and certainly for Peter in all his roughness and impulsiveness.

4.   Kindness is compassion and caring **whenever someone is in need.** Love and Kindness compel a Christian to reach out to others who are less fortunate. That is the Great Commission's order. Until a person has truly been transformed by the power of God, he will not be as sensitive to the needs of others as he should. Jesus very effectively used a parable to illustrate this point. He described the poor, helpless, beaten, and suffering man set upon by robbers on the road from Jerusalem to Jericho left by the side of the road to die. The irony of the story is obvious. First a priest came down the road but moved quickly to the other side to avoid any contact with the unfortunate traveler. Then a Levite saw the helpless, naked victim but also passed by him on the opposite side of the road. Both these so-called holy men were too preoccupied with their own importance and religion to bother with the suffering man, but a humble, despised Samaritan was touched with compassion and ministered to the helpless man. His act of Kindness included treating and binding up the man's wounds, putting him on his donkey, taking him to an inn of safety, and even leaving some money to pay for the man's recovery.

In describing the Good Samaritan, Jesus was perfectly characterizing Himself. He said He came to serve and not to be served and demonstrated this Kindness in many ways throughout His earthly ministry. Like the lowly Samaritan, Christ was far removed from the sanctimonious priest and Levite; He was likewise despised and rejected by religious leaders and His own society. He nevertheless pursued His purpose and reached out to many sick, helpless, and dying persons. Christ illustrated this type of kindness in the Sermon on the Mount when He spoke, *You have heard that it used to be said "Thou shalt love thy neighbor and hate thine enemy," but I tell you, Love your enemies, and pray for those who persecute you, so that you may be sons of your Heavenly Father. For he makes his sun rise upon evil men as well as good, and he sends his rain upon honest and dishonest men alike* (Matthew 5:45, Phillips). Kindness cannot be compromised; it is wise to be kind. Practical James puts it this way: *The wisdom that comes from God is first utterly pure, then peace-loving, gentle, approachable, full of tolerant thoughts and kindly actions, with no breath of favoritism or hint of hypocrisy* (James 3:17, Phillips).

5.   Finally, Kindness refers to reaching out to someone **in need physically, spiritually, or emotionally**. While the Good Samaritan ministered to another's physical need, Kindness also reaches out to a person who is suffering spiritually or emotionally. God created human beings as body, soul, and spirit, inseparably bound to Him as creations in His image. Sometimes we hurt physically, but more often our need is far more serious. Without realizing it, our mind, our will, and our emotions become sick and need a kind person to reach out to us. Because of the dysfunctional world in which we live, where children are neglected, separated from their parents, or abused, many grow up needing someone to show them kindness and love. Adults in our confusing society often bring baggage with them from childhood that results in anger, resentment, hatred, lack of self-esteem, and other emotional problems. Unfortunately, our prisons are filled with hurting people who know nothing of Kindness in their lives, so they exhibited behavior leading to acts of hostility, frustration, and violence. The only answer for someone whose life has been totally void of Love and Kindness is the transforming power of God to change any life yielded to Him. Christians hold the key to the rehabilitation of someone whose life has been ruined by sin. The Fruit of loving Kindness is a habit reserved for those who call Jesus Christ Lord and seek to live as He did. This kind of concern and care can change the world!

Beware of Manipulation Masquerading as Kindness

One further word about the world's perception of good deeds is necessary here. When we talk about the divine Fruit of Kindness, we are not talking about manipulation of others for personal gain. A discerning Christian will be able to detect false kindness or attempts by others to gain favor for personal advancement. Remember, Kindness is a holy habit resulting from a life of total surrender and dedication to Christ. One does not perform some act of kindness when his thoughts are on what he may receive in return for some good deed. Jacob cooked up a nice pot of tantalizing stew for Esau to see when he came in from hunting. Feigning kindness, Jacob offered a starving Esau some of his culinary specialty, but there was a catch. Esau had to give Jacob his birthright. Without thinking, a hungry Esau agreed. Jacob once again manipulated a situation for his own gain (Genesis 25:27). Delilah tricked Samson with her suave, fake kindness and convinced him to tell her the secret of his strength (Judges 16). This type of attention is the devil's way of deceiving people into believing a lie and falling for a false kindness.

In Shakespeare's tragedy *Macbeth*, he pictures a loyal, faithful general who is on his way to visit the current King Duncan at his castle in Scotland. General Macbeth's wife, however, has other plans for her husband. She thinks he ought to be king and uses some ill-advised prophecies to buoy him to kill Duncan and take over the throne. As she ruthlessly pursues the goal of getting the throne for her husband, she says, "Yet I do fear thy nature; It is too full o' th' milk of human kindness to catch the nearest way."[4] In other words, she must use manipulation to make him willing to murder the king while he sleeps. Against his better judgment and disposition Macbeth tries to take action but is too reluctant to follow through with the scheme. Lady Macbeth then finishes the deed by killing the king herself. Of course, they both pay the price for their actions and suffer tragic ends. With his uncanny insight into human nature Shakespeare illustrates what can happen in the life of a good person who yields to temptation and forsakes his God-given conscience. Kindness is not self-serving, manipulative, or destructive. Man apart from God is capable of most anything, and history bears this out. The real tragedy in life is to miss the real purpose for living – to offer love and kindness to others as Christ Himself exemplified.

Kindness or Correctness?

You have heard the statement, "It is better to be kind than correct." I remember some years ago a friend of mine discussing this in an article in a Christian magazine. He leaned toward kindness as appropriate in some situations rather than insisting upon absolute correctness at all times. Well, he received a number of letters from readers who disagreed with him vehemently. They argued that it is never permissible to compromise the truth of the scriptures, and a Christian must take a stand for his beliefs.

Herein is the dilemma for one truly transformed. Obviously there can be no compromise of God's infallible Word. We must defend it against heresy and apostasy. However, at the same time, a Christian must be sensitive to the Spirit in dealing with those who do not have the same insight and spiritual understanding as he. Dogged determination to be correct may indeed alienate someone who is sincerely trying to find the truth amid all the false teachings that abound today. Gently and kindly leading a friend to deeper understanding of repentance will be far more effective than harshly criticizing him for not believing what you believe. Jesus dealt with the Pharisees and Sadducees who insisted upon their correct interpretation of the law but lacked any real love or kindness in their relationships with others. As God personified, Jesus embodied the words Paul penned in II Corinthians 10:1, *Now I Paul myself beseech you by the meekness and gentleness of Christ* (KJV). He also writes in Romans 2:4, *Don't you realize that God's kindness is meant to lead you to repentance?* (Phillips) and Romans 11:22, *You must try to appreciate both the kindness and the strict justice of God. Those who fell experienced his justice, while you are experiencing his kindness, and will continue to do so as long as you do not abuse that kindness* (Phillips).

Another expression we use frequently is "Speaking the truth in love." The divine nature of the body of Christ (the Church) depends upon kind, loving relationships among believers. Too many times the Church of the Lord has been divided and fractured by Christians whose speech is void of kindness, resulting in alienation and hurt. Not too long ago I sat on a supersized 727 jet and marveled at the ability of a well-trained pilot to sit at the massive control panel of that huge aircraft, harness all that power, and guide the 200-passenger plane to a safe landing. No doubt that pilot had trained for many years to know what to do to land that plane, so it probably became second nature to him. In a similar fashion, using the instruments and Holy Spirit-inspired habits that God has given us, we truly transformed Christians need to realize that our cargo is precious and proceed with gentle, confident assurance that we can bring the Church to a safe destination.

Once again, "Kindness is an unselfish expression of compassionate concern and care whenever someone is in need physically, spiritually, or emotionally." There is no room in the life of a truly transformed Christian for arrogance, condescension, coldness, and indifference toward the needs of others. Kindness is one of the most essential qualities that distinguish a person as a follower of Christ. It is a visible attribute that draws men and women to a disciple and makes them want to be like Jesus.

Lord, I am so bound by my own desires
I find it hard to be kind and concerned
About those whose lives have no meaning
Or reason to love.
Sometimes I'd rather be correct or right
Than admit my attitude is wrong.
When you walked the dusty roads of life
You were always available and kind.
You reached out to the helpless and hopeless.
Help me to become like you.

CHAPTER EIGHT

Habit 6: Grasp God's Infinite Goodness

Luke 18:18, 19 – *Then one of the Jewish rulers put this question to him, "Master, I know that you are good; tell me, please, what must I do to be sure of eternal life." "I wonder why you call me good?" returned Jesus. "No one is good – only the one God"* (Phillips).

GOODNESS – The purity of spirit and moral excellence of motive and action that radiate from my life through the Holy Spirit as I obey God's Word.

Good vs. evil. Now there's a theme for you! Almost every dramatic novel or short story written has a protagonist and an antagonist, a hero and a villain. There's the cowboy in the white hat and the outlaw dressed in black, Gary Cooper in *High Noon,* the good guy and the bad guy. Where did all that confrontation begin? Somehow human beings know that certain behavior is right and other actions are wrong. We are made in the image of God, and God is totally, utterly Good! From the rebellion of Lucifer and his angels in heaven to the temptation of Eve by the serpent to Jesus confronting the devil in the wilderness, there has been a battle raging for the souls of men. Furthermore, that battle has become much more subtle and complex in a world of advanced information, technology, commercialization, and communication. Christians are bombarded with all kinds of conflicting messages through seemingly innocent television shows, movies, books, and advertisements. Young people especially have a tough time filtering out the junk and understanding the advanced tactics of the devil, who is the master deceiver. Evil masquerades under all kinds of costumes and lures well-meaning Christians into its trap. No wonder Goodness is a rarity in today's culture. Finding an example of a good person is difficult.

Granny Jones: An Example of Goodness

Come to think of it, I have known some good people whose paths have crossed mine. One of these individuals was Granny Jones. Mrs. Roxie Anna Cherry Jones was a fixture in the little community of Franklin Springs, Georgia, for many years. Granny, as everybody called her, had come to Franklin Springs in 1927 when her 30-year-old son, Byon A. Jones, was abruptly called upon to take over the struggling school as president. He had inherited a difficult assignment and served for only a couple of years before moving to another ministry, but Granny stayed. For many years students at Emmanuel College knew her as a powerful little prayer warrior who radiated goodness wherever she went.

When I was a student at Emmanuel in 1960, she lived in a little white frame house just yards away from the campus and attended the local Pentecostal Holiness Church. She was there every time the doors opened, sitting right up front, and when testimony time came (You remember those?), she was usually the first one up. I can still hear her saying in her soft, soothing voice as she swept her hand around the sanctuary, "I just love all of you students. I love everybody. I want you to know that I pray for you every day. God has been so good to me I can't thank Him enough. He is a wonderful Savior, and He supplies my every need!" I am told that one day a tornado was heading straight for the College campus, and Granny Jones started praying. Suddenly the tornado shifted its course across the highway on the opposite side of the campus, and every building was spared.

Then when I returned in 1969 as a member of the faculty at the College, she was still living in that little white frame house and still on fire for God. Her life and testimony never changed. She always exuded the Fruit of the Spirit in her actions and interactions with others in the community and the students at the College. What a powerhouse of prayer she was! You could just feel the Spirit of God when you talked to her or listened to her testimony. A simple, quiet woman, she never tried to call attention to herself but faithfully did what she could to further the kingdom of God in her way. I remember visiting her as she lay close to death in that little house and hearing her testimony for the last time. It was the same as always. She expressed her desire to see Jesus and soon went on to what must be a tremendous reward in heaven for her.

Even though she is gone physically, she left messages in stone. The little house has long since been demolished. Nothing remains but the stone columns and small porch her son made for the house and a beautiful little grassy area that was her front yard, now called Granny Jones' Park. During her life, almost every day you could see her out in the garden lovingly tending to her plants and flowers just as she cared for others. In her yard Granny had strategically placed some stepping stones from the street leading up to her porch. The stones are still there, but unfortunately, like so many meaningful things in life, they have become grown over with dirt and weeds, and are difficult to see. Without looking closely, the visitor to the garden would miss them. They are still there, though, and the messages on the stones are still readable. Granny put a little sermon on each stone, carefully etched into the rock so that the words would endure. The simple yet profound messages on those stones repeat her message of God's Goodness. The first one says, "Be Happy." The second, "Serve God." The third, "Have Faith." The next, "Pray Often." The next, "Be Kind." The next, "Don't worry." The next, "Keep Pure." And finally, the last one says, "God Bless You." Although the words in the stepping stones have become almost impossible to see, the message of Granny Jones will never fade. She was a good woman and a great example of the operation of the Fruit of the Spirit in a person's life.

Definition of Goodness

Of all the Fruit of the Spirit listed in Galatians 5:22-23, "Goodness" is perhaps the least understood. While we as human beings have the desire to do good works and use the term *good* to refer to the quality of a person with honorable intentions, Jesus in fact made the statement, *No one is good–only the one God* (Luke 18:19, Phillips). Actually what Christ is saying is that a person may be good in the natural sense of the word yet still lack the purity of motives and moral excellence that may only be present in the truly transformed life because God is infinitely and singularly good. Man's "goodness" is relative. Goodness in the absolute sense may be applied only to God. As Christ became God in the flesh, He was Goodness personified. He came to reproduce in us purity, cleanliness, and the goodness of God.

Again, quoting C. S. Lewis, "A Christian is not a man who never goes wrong, but a man who is enabled to repent and pick himself up and begin over again after each stumble—because the Christ-life is inside him, repairing him all the time, enabling him to repeat (in some degree) the kind of voluntary death which Christ Himself carried out. That is why the Christian is in a different position from other people who are trying to be good. They hope by being good, to please God if there is one; or—if they think there is not—at least they hope to deserve approval from good men. But the Christian thinks any good he does comes from the Christ-life inside him. He does not think God will love us because we are good, but that God will make us good because He loves us; just as the roof of a greenhouse does not attract the sun because it is bright, but becomes bright because the sun shines on it."[1]

Thus, our definition is this: **Goodness is the purity of spirit and moral excellence of motive and action that radiate from my life through the Holy Spirit as I obey God's Word.**

1. **Purity of spirit** characterizes Goodness. This is really uprightness of heart and life, faultlessness before the Lord. The Greek word here is *agathosune,* used in the New Testament to refer to regenerate persons. Another word, *eupoiia,* meaning to do good, is also sometimes used.[2] In other words, like other abstract nouns in the English language, the word *goodness* takes its meaning from the context in which it is used. Paul, reflecting on his own ministry and encouraging the Christians at Rome, stated, *I myself also am persuaded of you, my brethren, that ye also are full of goodness, filled with all knowledge, able also to admonish one another* (Romans 15:14, KJV). This purity of spirit that can be present in one's life is not natural, but it is natural for a Christian to have supernatural characteristics. The true transformation that comes into the life and spirit of a mere mortal is supernatural, beyond explanation. The attribute of Goodness is indeed a Fruit of the Spirit, a condition in the heart of a person that can come only because of the glorious Goodness inherent in the character of God. The habit of Goodness develops out of a heart of submission to the Holy Spirit and obedience to the Word of God.

2. Goodness is also **moral excellence of motive and action**. Here again in our definition the nouns "motive" and "action"

imply that Goodness is not just some emotional high or feeling of euphoria. It is God's character put into practice, something we do as a result of a supernatural change that has taken place in our soul and spirit. When God created man, His crowning achievement, in His own image, He put within man the potential for experiencing all the glorious attributes of the Father. Adam and Eve were divinely "good," but when they disobeyed God and sinned, that inherent goodness departed. From that point on, human beings have struggled to find meaning and moral excellence in a world left vulnerable to all of Satan's trickery and deception. Apart from the influence of God's Goodness in his being, man is victim to all the vices evil brings out in our fallen state—hatred, rebellion, strife, jealousy, lust, greed, bitterness, and selfishness. In the Old Testament the Israelites experienced signs and evidences of the glory of God as He reminded them of their helplessness apart from His divine intervention, but they did not understand the totality of His will and direction. For many years the Ark of the Covenant symbolized God's glory in the tent of meeting and the tabernacle. The people of Israel partially grasped the glory as God moved through the presence of the Ark, but they still were in darkness.

During their 40 years of wandering, the Children of Israel constantly complained and rebelled against the will and direction of God. Knowing their humanity and departure from Goodness, God gave to Moses the Ten Commandments, ten guidelines for human behavior that delineated specific areas of conduct in relationships with God and others. Man has always had a tendency to question and resist God's divine order and purpose. However, the Holy Spirit can transform that spirit of resentment, bitterness, and rebellion into a life of moral excellence of motive and action. Obviously, it is good to have a list of dos and don'ts such as the Ten Commandments, and they are still just as relevant today as they were for the Israelites. Nonetheless, a truly transformed Christian does not depend upon a set or rules or list of prohibitions for his moral and spiritual purity. He has been supernaturally transformed by the power of God back to the state of innocence and holiness God intended when He created Adam and Eve. Jesus Christ alone could bring about the restoration of the glory of God into the lives of mankind through His death and resurrection, the supreme sacrifice for the sake of Goodness.

3.   As a result of the Fruit of Goodness operating in my motives and actions, purity of spirit and moral excellence **radiate from my life**. Goodness will shine forth. The difference between moral purity and moral corruption or immorality is as clear as night from day. Isaiah proclaimed, *The people that walked in darkness have seen a great light: they that dwell in the land of the shadow of death, upon them hath the light shined* (Isaiah 9:2, KJV). Again he shouts, *I will make darkness light before them and crooked things straight* (Isaiah 42:16, KJV), and *Arise, shine; for thy light is come, and the glory of the Lord is risen upon thee* (Isaiah 60:1, KJV). The Psalmist declared, *The Lord is my light and my salvation, whom shall I fear* (27:1, KJV), and *He shall bring forth thy righteousness as the light, and thy judgment as the noonday* (37:6, KJV).

Of course, the radiant light prophesied by Isaiah and others was Jesus Christ, of whom Luke declared, *Whereby the dayspring from on high hath visited us, to give light to them that sit in darkness and in the shadow of death, to guide our feet into the way of peace* (1:78, 79, KJV), and John reiterated, *In him was life; and the life was the light of men. And the light shineth in darkness; and the darkness comprehended it not* (John 1:4, 5, KJV). Jesus first declared, *I am the light of the world: he that followeth me shall not walk in darkness, but shall have the light of life* (John 8:12, KJV). Then he added, *Ye are the light of the world. A city that is set on a hill cannot be hid. Neither do men light a candle, and put it under a bushel, but on a candlestick; and it giveth light unto all that are in the house. Let your light so shine among men, that they may see your good works, and glorify your Father which is in heaven* (Matt. 5:14-16, KJV). Paul echoes this revelation in II Corinthians 4:3-6: *The spirit of this world has blinded the minds of those who do not believe, and prevents the light of the glorious Gospel of Christ, the image of God, from shining on them. For it is Christ Jesus the Lord whom we preach, not ourselves; we are your servants for his sake. God, who first ordered light to shine in darkness, has flooded our hearts with his light. We now can enlighten men only because we can give them the knowledge of the glory of God, as we see it in the face of Jesus Christ* (Phillips).

In Ephesians 5:5-13 Paul further clarifies the situation of light vs.

darkness: *For of this much you can be quite certain: that neither the immoral nor the dirty-minded nor the covetous man (which latter is, in effect, worshiping a false god) has any inheritance in the kingdom of Christ and of God. Don't let anyone fool you on this point, however plausible his argument. It is these very things which bring down the wrath of God upon the disobedient. Have nothing to do with men like that – once you were "darkness" but now you are "light." Live then as children of the light. The light produces in men quite the opposite of sins like these – everything that is wholesome and good and true. Let your lives be living proofs of the things which please God. Steer clear of the activities of darkness; let your lives show by contrast how dreary and futile these things are. (You know the sort of things I mean – to detail their secret doings is really too shameful.) For light is capable of "showing up" everything for what it really is. It is even possible (after all, it happened with you!) for light to turn the thing it shines upon into light also* (Phillips). The King James Version of verse 9 states more directly what we are saying, *For the fruit of the Spirit is in all goodness and righteousness and truth.* Therefore, Spiritual darkness is the absence of God's Goodness and glory in a person's life. Goodness, then, is radiating the love of God through our lives every day.

4.   Goodness radiates from my life **through the Holy Spirit**. In the familiar passage of Romans 7:18-25 Paul attempts to explain the dilemma we humans have trying to be good within ourselves but not succeeding. *For I know that in me (that is, in my flesh,) dwelleth no good thing: for to will is present with me; but how to perform that which is good I find not. For the good that I would I do not: but the evil which I would not, that I do. Now if I do that I would not, it is no more I that do it, but sin that dwelleth in me. I find then a law, that, when I would do good, evil is present with me. For I delight in the law of God after the inward man: But I see another law in my members, warring against the law of my mind, and bringing me into captivity to the law of sin which is in my members. O wretched man that I am! Who shall deliver me from the body of this death? I thank God through Jesus Christ our Lord* (KJV). In other words Paul is saying that he often finds that he has the desire to do good within himself but not the power! That's where the Holy Spirit must

come in and illuminate the mind, soul, and spirit of a person to the reality of Jesus Christ, the only answer. The Holy Spirit enables us to overcome the domination of sin in our human nature. The law of sin and death drags us down, but another law lifts us up beyond ourselves, the law of the spirit of life and light in Christ Jesus.

What we must grasp here is that Goodness in a man is not inherent. Only submission to the Holy Spirit's guidance may produce good fruit in the life of a person whose life has been supernaturally changed by the power of God. Paul realized that without Christ he was doomed to suffer from evil thoughts, harmful actions, and continual internal conflict. The 18th-century Romanticists extolled the virtues of man, who, in their thinking, was within himself basically good and capable of rising to new heights of goodness and glory. As knowledge of the primitive world of African tribes expanded with ships sailing to then unknown parts of the world, they cited the so-called innocence and purity of the "Noble Savage." (Just like the romantic stories of Tarzan, these accounts were highly imaginative.) Thus the humanistic heresy of today was revived. Modern humanists still contend that man does not need God; he is born good and must pull himself up by his own boot-straps and make something of his life. What the Bible says, and what history has proven to be true, is that man left to his own inclinations is basically evil apart from God's grace and power to save. There is no Goodness in life until a man has yielded to the convicting power of the Holy Spirit and sees his utter failure and helplessness apart from God. Jesus put to rest the idea of man's independent potential for Goodness in Luke 6:43-45, where He says, *It is impossible for a good tree to produce bad fruit—as impossible as it is for a bad tree to produce good fruit. Do not men know what a tree is by its fruit? You cannot pick figs from briars, or gather a bunch of grapes from a blackberry bush. A good man produces good things from the good stored up in his heart, and a bad man produces evil things from his own stores of evil. For a man's words will always express what has been treasured in his heart* (Phillips). He was Goodness personified and demonstrated the love and goodness of God through his ultimate sacrifice on Calvary. Then He rose again to bring eternal hope and to return Goodness to the world forever!

5. Then, the final clause of our definition indicates that Goodness shines forth through my life only **as I obey God's Word**. Strength to overcome evil and to do good is possible only as we continue in the Word. Again, in that powerful illustration of the vine and the branches in John 15, Jesus said, *If you live your life in me, and my words live in your hearts, you can ask for whatever you like and it will come true for you. This is how my Father will be glorified—in your becoming fruitful and being my disciples* (vs. 7, 8, Phillips). In another unforgettable statement He says, *If you continue in my word, then are ye my disciples indeed; And ye shall know the truth, and the truth shall make you free* (John 8:31, 32, KJV). The Psalmist David declared, *Thy word have I hid in my heart that I might not sin against thee* (KJV), and *Thy word is a lamp unto my* feet *and a light unto my path* (KJV). As one submits to the inspiration of the Holy Spirit's guidance in his life, the Word of God continually refreshes and energizes his walk with the Lord. The habits developed supernaturally within the believer are enhanced powerfully by the continuous illumination that comprehension of the Word brings. In fact, all the Fruit of the Spirit are developed and enhanced by concentrating upon the words provided in the Bible for our edification. The habit of daily prayer and devotional time is crucial to the maturation process in the life of a Christian. Being good is superior to doing good!

A Word about Sanctification

Now then, our definition of Goodness is "the purity of spirit and the moral excellence and action that radiate from my life through the Holy Spirit as I obey God's Word." We have established that Goodness in man can come only as a result of a divine transformation that takes place at the moment a person yields his or her life to Christ and acknowledges Christ as Savior and Lord. Through His vicarious suffering, sacrifice, death, and resurrection, Jesus restored the glory and Goodness of the Father into the beings of those who would obediently take up their cross and follow Him. Only after this glorious, miraculous transformation has taken place in a person's life can he or she establish holy habits like Goodness. Being good is not in the nature of fallen man. That is really the overriding problem of man separated from God. If we were all basically good, there would be no need for laws, policemen, jails, or prohibitions with consequences for evil actions. Only redeemed, transformed Christians can provide the light the world needs through habits of the Fruit of the Spirit demonstrated daily in their relationships. As Jesus pointed out, we are to be in the world but not of the world.

Even though I grew up in a holiness-preaching denomination, for many years I did not understand what holiness or "sanctification" meant. We were taught that somehow after a person confesses his sins, asks Jesus to come into his heart, and is "saved" or "born again," there is another, deeper experience to follow to seek specifically, a "second definite work of grace." Much confusion has continued to surround the teaching of sanctification, and words like *initial*, *instantaneous*, *progressive*, and *entire* have been a part of the description of what happens in a person's life when he is sanctified.

Furthermore, holiness of heart and life has been elusive for Christians trying within themselves to merit God's favor. During my formative years I viewed sanctification and holiness from a negative perspective as something impossible to accomplish, and we concentrated more on what holiness forbade us to do than the positive, transformational change that takes place when a person becomes truly capable of experiencing the holiness and Goodness of God in his own soul and spirit by faith. Our misguided perception of holiness gave us an inferiority complex growing up with a list of prohibitions such as no movies, no dances, no make-up, no mixed bathing (actually no swimming with the opposite sex), no rock and roll music, no working on Sunday, etc. I'll stop here, for I am no doubt dating myself. These were simply tangible indicators of one's internal separation from the world's sin after he has become a Christian and emphasized the outward evidences of what God has done to purify the life of a believer. Our holiness forefathers were no doubt sincere in their teaching and preaching and attempted to delineate the differences that Christ makes when He transforms a person. In our so-called enlightened 21st-century views, these early proponents of holiness were too strict, misinformed, ignorant, and uneducated. However, if you think about what our society and country have come to in moral deterioration and blatant disregard for God's holy nature, maybe we could use a little more of our predecessors' preaching. They were, in fact, not that far off in their insistence upon holiness.

Actually our definition of Goodness is very close to what the true meaning of sanctification is. The saving grace of God is sufficient for anyone who confesses Jesus as Savior and Lord of his life. At the moment of conversion, one is potentially restored to the place of security and eternal salvation made possible by the blood of Jesus on the cross. The full measure of the Fruit of the Spirit is possible to all who believe. However, there is a maturation process that involves prayer, daily commitment, continued sensitivity to the Spirit, and increased awareness of God's divine guidance in our everyday lives. As a Christian grows in his awareness of his potential in developing Christlike character, he perceives the need to call upon the Lord for a further purification and holiness of heart and life. That is the "instantaneous" aspect of the experience of sanctification. At the same time, one must recognize that holiness and Goodness are attributes of God, and we must appropriate His nature as we live and breathe on this earth. That, then, is the "progressive" aspect of holiness. We have pointed out earlier that the Fruit of the Spirit work in tandem and are produced in a person's life much like the fruit ripens on the tree or vine. The love of God as exemplified in the life of Christ is reproduced supernaturally in a human being by faith and through the inspiration of the Holy Spirit, who is with us always.

Goodness, Purity, and Light

Now we have been using the analogy of light vs. darkness to describe Goodness as it is a part of God's nature. Actually the Holy Spirit is that Light God puts within us, and He expects that light to shine forth in our lives. As He Himself acknowledged, Jesus was that Light personified and promised to leave with us the Holy Spirit that will radiate through us. Goodness is evidenced by our becoming bearers of the light of the knowledge of God to a pagan world. Thus, all the Fruit of the Spirit, including Goodness (or holiness), become second nature to us and are evidenced daily in our interactions with others and our relationship with the Lord. In I John 1:5-7 the writer beautifully proclaims, *Here, then, is the message we heard him give. GOD IS LIGHT, and not the faintest shadow of darkness can exist in him. Consequently, if we were to say that we enjoyed fellowship with him and still went on living in darkness, we should be both telling and living a lie. But if we really are living in the same light in which he eternally exists, then we have true fellowship with each other, and the blood he shed for us keeps us clean from any and every sin* (Phillips). Wow! That sums it up powerfully, doesn't it? Peter also adds his inspired insight, *It is for you now to demonstrate the goodness of him who has called you out of darkness into his amazing light. In the past you were not 'a people' at all: now you are the people of God. In the past you had no experience of his mercy, but now it is intimately yours* (I Peter 2:9, 10; Phillips).

True Goodness vs. Hypocrisy

Before we leave this discussion of what constitutes true Goodness, we must note that, as with all the Fruit of the Spirit, man manufactures a fake or counterfeit characteristic. Of course, deception and hypocrisy are favorite tricks of the devil as he seeks to destroy the true Fruit in our lives. As we have noted previously, with Satan's help human beings try to imitate God's miraculous work of grace, a condition leading to a false impression of Goodness fabricated to deceive others. Man alone cannot eradicate darkness although he desperately tries. Humanism, situational ethics, postmodernism, and other atheistic teachings offer empty explanations for man's condition apart from the admission of his dependence upon a divine Creator and loving Father. The bottom line is the fact that, no matter how hard he tries, man can never be good enough to make it to heaven. That is only possible because of the divinely imparted Goodness of God made possible by the death and resurrection of Jesus.

There is also a danger of the organized Church substituting good works and superficial programs for the true spreading of the light of God's Goodness to a lost world. In all the success of some congregations to show the world their ability to build huge, impressive sanctuaries and to impress others with their prosperity, one has to wonder if this is the light God really intends for us to share. To the lukewarm church at Laodicea John warned, *While you say, "I am rich, I have prospered, and there is nothing I need," you have no eyes to see that you are wretched, pitiable, poverty-stricken, blind and naked. My advice to you is to buy from me that gold which is purified in the furnace so that you may be rich, and white garments to wear so that you may hide the shame of your nakedness, and salve to put on your eyes to make you see. All those whom I love I correct and discipline. Therefore, shake off your complacency and repent. See I stand knocking at the door. If anyone listens to my voice and opens the door, I will go into his house and dine with him, and he with me* (Revelation 3:15, Phillips). God abhors hypocrisy as much as blatant sin. He alone is God; He will not share His glory with anyone else.

The Habit of Goodness

Now, our definition of Goodness is "the purity of spirit and moral excellence of motive and action that radiate from my life through the Holy Spirit as I obey God's Word." What the world needs to see coming from a truly transformed Christian is Goodness. In his letter to Titus, Paul reminded him, *But when the kindness of God our Savior and his love appeared, he saved us—not by virtue of any moral achievements of ours, but by the cleansing power of a new birth and the moral renewal of the Holy Spirit, which he gave us so generously through Jesus Christ our Savior. The result is that we are acquitted by his grace, and can look forward to inheriting life for evermore. This is solid truth: I want you to speak about these matters with absolute certainty, so that those who have believed in God may concentrate upon a life of goodness* (Titus 3:4-8, Phillips). Jesus went about doing good, and we are to emulate His character. One cannot imitate God's Goodness by simply doing some good things for others. There is an awareness of right and wrong in every human being's soul. Through custom, environment, and training, children learn to do good things. On the other hand, sin has created a strong temptation, often embellished by a godless culture, to do evil things. Many times men yield to their baser instincts and circumvent God's intended purpose for their lives. As a result, our society is suffering from overcrowded prisons, rampant crime, abused and abandoned children, racial tensions, apathetic workers, and other evidences of a world apart from God. The only real remedy for this tendency of man to sin is the infusion of the power of God's goodness, purity, holiness, and light into the life of a person truly and miraculously transformed by the Holy Spirit. Christians are the only catalyst for 21st-century America; we must be salt and light to our generation!

Great God of infinite goodness and light
Reproduce in me your divinity.
I am too prone to darkness and gloom
When you desire to shine forth in me.
Throughout the utter blackness that
Blinded us from the Truth
A Lamb illuminated the night in Bethlehem
And Goodness came to earth.

CHAPTER NINE

Habit 7: Find Faithfulness First

Psalm 89:1-2 – *I will sing of the Lord's great love forever; with my mouth I will make your faithfulness known through all generations. I will declare that your love stands firm forever, that you established your faithfulness in heaven itself* (NIV).

FAITHFULNESS – The determination to submit constantly and unfailingly my future to God through obedient loyalty, sincerity, and responsibility.

If one is to emulate the character of Christ is his life, he must put Faithfulness at the top of the list of holy habits to guide his actions and decisions. If the other Fruit of the Spirit are to be evident in my life, I must first find Faithfulness to be a part of my daily motivation. Without it, there will be a vast void in my endeavor to live victoriously. Nouns like *loyalty, truthfulness, availability, endurance, diligence, determination, reliability, trustworthiness, steadfastness,* and *responsibility,* all synonymous with Faithfulness, are sadly becoming archaic words in our language, and faithful Christians are hard to find. I can remember the day in America when a man was as good as his word, and daily business was conducted with trust and truthfulness. Not so today! In a day of enlightenment, advanced technology, and rapid transmission of information, those with sinister motives have taken over the business world. Every day charlatans prey upon innocent victims trying to relieve them of their life savings. The American way has become "get someone else before they get you." We have learned to trust no one and to beware of all schemes and trickery. Faithfulness in business, in families, and in churches is a lost cause. The general lack of faithfulness in our day has resulted in the necessity for multiplying laws, creating more government agencies to enforce these laws, and higher taxes to law-abiding citizens to help pay for these agencies. The situation makes a truly transformed Christian long for the day when Christ shall reign in righteousness and love!

Now before I get too far here, let me say that I know some outstanding men and women who live godly lives, and I have had the privilege of working with some of the most dedicated, humble, self-sacrificing, and faithful people anywhere. When the Fruit of Faithfulness is working in a person's life, it is quite evident. Two special men come to mind here. I had the privilege of working with Dr. Kirk Hartsfield for many years. He was dean of men at Emmanuel College when I enrolled as a freshman, and he made a powerful impact on the lives of all the residents of the dorm he supervised. He also taught a number of classes and completed his doctorate in Education with honors. From that role he moved to the position of dean of students and rescued many a student from calamity year after year. Then he moved to the academic arena as academic dean and guided the College through several accreditation cycles and a move to add a four-year liberal arts curriculum to the programs offered. He also served as executive vice president. A professional in every way, Dr. Hartsfield performed his responsibilities with dignity, honor, and effectiveness in whatever role he played without expecting any praise or recognition. He was faithful and consistent at all times in his execution of his duties until his retirement and is admired by students, faculty, and alumni for his integrity and character.

Another colleague who could be counted upon to do his best was Ed Henson. Ed Henson is one of the most admired and revered persons ever associated with Emmanuel College. He also served as residence director and dean of students for over 25 years. In spite of a disability that hampered his walking, he could move around more quickly than anyone on campus, and students knew he had an uncanny ability to find out what was going on in the residence halls and on campus. The stories of his wisdom and interaction with students are numerous and hilarious at times. Mr. Henson retired several years ago and is still recognized by many alumni of the

College as the one who helped them succeed. When I think of faithful men, I automatically recall the names of Kirk Hartsfield and Ed Henson. We are fortunate to encounter such people along the way who illustrate not only faithfulness but all the Fruit of the Spirit in their daily actions.

Faithfulness an Attribute of God

Actually the Fruit of Faithfulness is a characteristic of God Himself. Deuteronomy 7:9a verifies this: *Know therefore that the Lord thy God, he is God, the faithful God* (KJV). Jeremiah proclaimed, *It is of the Lord's mercies that we are not consumed, because his compassions fail not. They are new every morning: great is thy faithfulness* (Lamentations 3:22-23, KJV). In Psalm 36:5 David proclaims, *Thy mercy, O Lord, is in the heavens; and thy faithfulness reacheth unto the clouds* (KJV). Then in the 89th Psalm the writer declares, *I will sing of the mercies of the Lord forever: with my mouth will I make known thy faithfulness to all generations. For I have said, Mercy shall be built up forever: thy faithfulness shalt thou establish in the very heavens* (Psalm 89:1, 2; KJV). He goes on to add, *And the heavens shall praise thy wonders, O Lord: thy faithfulness also in the congregation of the saints* (vs. 5), and *O Lord God of hosts, who is a strong Lord like unto thee? or to thy faithfulness round about thee?* (vs. 8) In that same chapter God, who is speaking of King David's leadership of the people of Israel, says, *But my faithfulness and my mercy shall be with him: and in my name shall his horn be exalted* (vs. 24), and *Nevertheless my lovingkindness will I not utterly take from him, nor suffer my faithfulness to fail* (vs. 33). God's faithfulness is seen in his dealing with the Church in Smyrna in Revelation 2:10, where He declares, *Fear none of those things which thou shalt suffer: behold the devil shall cast some of you into prison, that ye may be tried; and ye shall have tribulation ten days: be thou faithful unto death, and I will give thee a crown of life* (KJV), and in 17:14, where He describes the last-ditch attempts of Satan to destroy the Church, *These shall make war with the Lamb, and the Lamb shall overcome them: for he is Lord of lords, and King of kings: and they that are with him are called, and chosen, and faithful* (KJV). Hallelujah to the faithful Lamb!

Jesus Was Ever Faithful

The perfect illustration of Faithfulness is, of course, Jesus himself. He repeatedly reminded his disciples that his sole purpose in coming to earth was to do the will of his Heavenly Father. When the disciples were concerned about his not eating, Jesus replied, *My food is doing the will of him who sent me and finishing the work he has given me* (John 4:34, Phillips). Again, in John 5:30, He responded, *By myself I can do nothing. As I hear, I judge, and my judgment is true because I do not live to please myself but to do the will of the Father who sent me* (Phillips). Further, in John 8:29-30, He answers the question of his deity: *When you have lifted up the Son of Man, then you will realize that I am who I say I am, and that I do nothing on my own authority but speak simply as my Father has taught me. The one who sent me is with me now: the Father has never left me alone, for I always do what pleases him* (Phillips). Then the writer of Hebrews sums up Christ's Faithfulness: *So then, my brothers in holiness who share the highest of all callings, I want you to think of the messenger and High Priest of the faith we hold, Christ Jesus. See him as faithful to the charge God gave him, and compare him with Moses who also faithfully discharged his duty in the household of God* (Phillips); and *It was imperative that he should be made like his brothers in nature, if he were to become a High Priest both compassionate and faithful to the things of God, and at the same time able to make atonement for the sins of the people* (Hebrews 2:17-18, Phillips). Then the writer gives a final proclamation of our High Priest: *Seeing that we have a great High Priest who has entered the inmost Heaven, Jesus the Son of God, let us hold firmly to our faith. For we have no superhuman High Priest to whom our weaknesses are unintelligible—he himself has shared fully in all our experience of temptation, except that he never sinned* (Hebrews 4:14-16, Phillips). Indeed we have a faithful High Priest who is constantly interceding for us.

Definition of Faithfulness

Now let's look at our definition. **Faithfulness is the determination to submit constantly and unfailingly my future to God through obedient loyalty, sincerity, and responsibility.**

1. Faithfulness is **determination**. It requires stickability and endurance. There is a certain amount of trust in God that has to be present in the midst of discouragement. Bill Gothard's definition of determination is "purposing to accomplish God's goals in God's time regardless of the opposition.[1] The Greek word for Faithfulness is *pistis,* meaning "believing, trusting, relying."[2] John Swails, a

noted Bible scholar and teacher, has said many times, "There is a monotony to righteousness," and that is true. At times in a truly transformed Christian's life he or she simply must be faithful to what is right and trust God. Not every aspect of life is going to be pleasant always, and durability, constancy, and diligence will work to get one through the tough times. Faithfulness is related to Love, Patience, and the other Fruit of the Spirit in that it serves God without expecting anything in return and does not rely upon human approval for affirmation. Paul wrote to the Christians in Thessalonica, *We are always thankful as we pray for you all, for we never forget that your faith has meant solid achievement, your love has meant hard work, and the hope that you have in our Lord Jesus Christ means sheer dogged endurance in the life that you live before God, the Father of us all* (I Thess. 1:2-3; Phillips). The habit of faithful trust is not an easy one to master, but the Holy Spirit can inspire and invigorate a life to accomplish supernatural things in Christ. Peter warns, *Be sober, be vigilant; because your adversary the devil, as a roaring lion, walketh about, seeking whom he may devour: Whom resist stedfast in the faith, knowing that the same afflictions are accomplished in your brethren that are in the world* (I Peter 5:8-9; KJV). Determination is essential to allow the Fruit of the Spirit to work in my life.

2.   Then Faithfulness is the determination to submit **constantly and unfailingly** my future to God. We use the two adverbs *constantly* and *unfailingly* in the definition because they have different connotations. *Constantly* means "without interruption, continuously, without fail" and implies the passing of time. It requires my continuous reliance upon my trust in God to see me through. *Unfailingly* suggests that Faithfulness is a matter of my will to follow Christ and my mental awareness of the need to rely upon His will and direction at all times. Developing the habit of Faithfulness requires daily dependence upon the power of the Holy Spirit to keep me in a constant and an unfailing commitment to follow God's purpose for my life.

3.   I must constantly and unfailingly **submit my future to God** in order to be Faithful. In his book *The Seven Habits of Highly Effective People*, one of the habits Stephen Covey talks about is,

"Begin with the End in Mind."[3] At the beginning of that chapter, he asks the reader to go through a very stirring exercise. Picture yourself at the end of your life. You are lying in a casket at your funeral. Imagine the final words of those who come by to view your body. What are they saying about you? That's a sobering thought, isn't it? While the idea of beginning with the end in mind is important in the business sense, it is even more essential for a Christian to think ahead and realize that God has the future under control. Faithfulness requires a forward kind of thinking and trust in God's Word. Man apart from God finds it extremely difficult if not impossible to be faithful even in the small things of daily life, and where there is lack of dependability there is unpredictable conduct and no direction. That is why so many people in modern America and around the world are drifting aimlessly through life and have no real goal or driving force to give them direction. They are as lost as a ship without a compass or a traveler without a roadmap. Habitually faithful people just believe that God is leading and guiding them each day and give the future to Him. Of course, this looking to the future includes a steadfast belief in the fact that Christ is coming back to earth to claim His Church. That reality enhances Faithfulness.

4.   Faithfulness is possible only through **obedient** loyalty, sincerity, and responsibility. Here the key word is the adjective *obedient*. There is a direct correlation between obedience and Faithfulness. Without acknowledging the infallibility and inerrancy of God's Word, man has nothing upon which to rely. In fact, obedience is essential in order for the Fruit of the Spirit to operate in my life at all. The Holy Spirit cannot carry out His kingdom work through your or my life unless we are obedient to His promptings as related to God's Word. The disobedience of the Children of Israel resulted from their unbelief, a factor that kept them from entering into the Promised Land. Time and time again God tried to warn them about their attitudes and lack of trust, but they did not listen. Their lack of obedience produced habits of human failure and frailty. We are no different today. The writer of Hebrews warns, *Take heed, brethren, lest there be in any of you an evil heart of unbelief, in departing from the living God. But exhort one another daily, while it is called*

to day; lest any of you be hardened through the deceitfulness of sin. For we are made partakers of Christ, if we hold the beginning of our confidence stedfast unto the end (Hebrews 3:12-14; KJV).

5.   Now Faithfulness requires **loyalty**. Bill Gothard defines loyalty as "using difficult times to demonstrate my commitment to God and to those whom He has called me to serve."[4] Loyalty is largely a lost commodity today. A faithful Christian is unwavering in his loyalty and commitment to the cause of Christ. Hence he is also loyal to his family, friends, and brothers and sisters in the faith. The entire economic future of the United States is in jeopardy because of the lack of loyalty among employees who simply see their jobs as necessities to have the money to be able to live their lives of luxury and ease. Even in the Church there are unfaithful servants who take advantage of their positions to advance their own selfish ambitions. God is not pleased with this kind of behavior. Loyalty also implies truthfulness in my relationships with others, availability to perform whatever tasks God gives me in life, and a fidelity to my family and Church. The Old Testament word (from which our "amen" is derived) can be translated either as "truth" or "faithfulness." That places the unfaithful man and the untruthful man in the same category. Proverbs 12:22 says, *Lying lips are abomination to the Lord: but they that deal truly* [i.e., with faithfulness] *are his delight* (KJV). Thus, integrity, truthfulness, and loyalty are all included in Faithfulness.

6.   Faithfulness also requires **sincerity**. There can be no greater habit related to Faithfulness than sincerity. Bill Gothard's definition of sincerity is "eagerness to do what is right with transparent motives."[5] Hypocrisy is the worst form of unfaithfulness and is repulsive to God. Unfortunately there are those even in the Christian world who appear to be faithful but have a halfheartedness about completing whatever task they have to perform either in the Church or in a secular job. Both are abominations. In I Corinthians 4:1-5 Paul talks about this: *You should look upon us as ministers of Christ, as trustees of the secrets of God. And it is a prime requisite in a trustee that he should prove worthy of his trust. But, as a matter of fact, it matters very little to me what you, or any man, thinks of me—I don't even value my opinion of myself. For I might be quite*

ignorant of any fault in myself—but that doesn't justify me before God. My only true judge is God himself. The moral of this is that we should make no hasty or premature judgments. When the Lord comes he will bring into the light of day all that at present is hidden in darkness, and he will expose the secret motives of men's hearts. Then shall God himself give each man his share of praise (Phillips). Insincerity and hypocrisy will be exposed as God separates the sheep from the goats. Faithfulness and sincerity go hand in hand.

7. Finally, Faithfulness carries with it **responsibility**. Responsibility involves consciously and habitually following through with whatever task or assignment I am given to complete, no matter how trivial or menial it may be. God expects Faithfulness in the small things, and He will reward us with greater responsibilities as we carry out the everyday duties that present themselves. In His parable of Luke 12:35-40 Jesus illustrates this point: *You must be ready, dressed, and have your lamps alight, like men who wait to welcome their lord and master on his return from the wedding feast, so that when he comes and knocks at the door they may open it for him at once. Happy are the servants whom their lord finds on the alert when he arrives. I assure you that he will then take off his outer clothes, make them sit down to dinner, and come and wait on them. And if he should come just after midnight or in the very early morning and find them still on the alert, their happiness is assured. But be certain of this, that if the householder had known the time when the burglar would come, he would not have let his house be broken into. So you must be on the alert, for the Son of Man is coming at a time when you may not expect him* (Phillips). When Peter asked the Lord the meaning of the parable, Jesus replied, *Well, who will be the faithful, sensible steward whom his master will put in charge of his household to give them their supplies at the proper time? Happy is the servant if his master finds him so doing when he returns. I tell you he will promote him to look after all his property* (Luke 12:42-44, Phillips).

On the other hand, lack of discipline results in irresponsibility. In the same passage of Luke 12, Jesus continues, *But suppose the servant says to himself, "My master takes his time about returning," and then begins to beat the men and women servants and to eat and drink and get drunk, that servant's lord and master will return suddenly and unexpectedly, and he will punish him severely and send him to share the penalty of the unfaithful. The slave who knows his master's plan but does not get ready or act upon it will be severely punished, but the servant who did not know the plan, though he has done wrong, will be let off lightly. Much will be expected from the one who has been given much, and the more a man is trusted, the more people will expect of him* (Luke 12:45-48, Phillips). Many a student has failed a course because of lack of discipline; many an employee has lost his job because of laziness. A Christian will never reach the potential that God has for him until he has mastered responsibility. As always, Christ is the best example of the Fruit of Faithfulness encompassing loyalty, sincerity, and responsibility. He never wavered from His heavenly purpose. He knew what He had to do. In spite of the temptation to take the easy way out, He prayed to the Father, "Not my will but thy will be done." He was loyal to the Father and to His disciples, He was truly transparent in all ways, and He took upon Himself the ultimate responsibility of going to the cross to die for you and me. Now that is Faithfulness.

Faithfulness in Marriage

As we have mentioned before (Chapter III, "Love"), marriage is a mirror of God's character. As Christ, the Bridegroom, is looking for His true bride, the Church, the Fruit of the Spirit must be evident in the union between a man and a woman. Nowhere in our daily living out the Fruit of the Spirit should these virtues be more observable than in our relationships with our spouses. As in most areas of our behavior, the habit of Faithfulness is essential for a marriage to succeed. Probably the single most detrimental crisis for the Christian Church today is the lack of loyalty and Faithfulness among Christian husbands and wives. Statistics reveal that in contemporary America, divorces among Christian couples are just as high as for non-Christians. Something is dreadfully wrong if that is true. Husbands become too consumed by their anti-Christian culture and succumb to the temptations of a self-centered, self-gratifying nation. Wives also become victims to a soap-opera lifestyle and are absorbed by trying to keep up with their neighbor's possessions.

In any marriage, communication, honesty, transparency of motive, and faithfulness are the secrets of success. Like anything else worthwhile, marriage takes work and mutual respect. In the chapter on Meekness we will talk about yielding one's rights, but mentioning that factor here is important as well. Marriage, as the cliché goes, is not a 50-50 proposition but 100% from both partners! Just as a truly transformed Christian has submitted his or her life completely to Christ, in marriage the husband and the wife must be willing to yield their rights in favor of the other. Spiritually they have become one, and mentally and emotionally that must happen as well. For many men, particularly, this factor is difficult to absorb, but life in the Spirit is so much more productive when marriage is a model of the operation of the Fruit of the Spirit.

Then parents need to be faithful toward their children. A sad commentary on our times is the fact that many children grow up in an abusive or dysfunctional family without love and faithfulness demonstrated. Rampant divorce has separated children from one or both of their parents, leaving innocent boys and girls to fend for themselves in a cruel, sinful world. Blessed indeed are the children of parents who love and care for them without fail and who are faithful to them.

Faithfulness in the Church

Now before we leave the discussion of Faithfulness, we must apply the same definition to our church attendance and involvement. In his discussion of our liberty to approach the Father through Jesus Christ the Son in Hebrews 10, the writer states, *In this confidence let us hold on to the hope that we profess without the slightest hesitation—for he is utterly dependable—and let us think of one another and how we can encourage one another to love and do good deeds. And let us not hold aloof from our Church meetings, as some do. Let us do all we can to help one another's faith, and this the more earnestly as we see the final day drawing ever nearer* (Hebrews 10:23-25, Phillips).

In this age of advanced technology, instant communication, and multimedia visibility, the truly transformed Christian must not forsake the opportunities to reach out to fellow believers and to join in corporate worship to God. Watching a televangelist at home is good for those who are unable to go to church, but there is no excuse for an able-bodied Christian not to assemble for worship with his friends and family. Actually, the true test of the Fruit of the Spirit working in the life of a Christian comes with relationships, both in the church family and outside the four walls of the sanctuary. The truly transformed believer is going to be the same whenever he or she interacts with fellow church members or with non-believers. The Holy Spirit's power to transform continues throughout life and in all circumstances, regardless of the type of contacts we make daily. If the Fruit is there, our coworkers will see it, our fellow church members will see it, our friends will see it, and the world will see it. Faithfulness, consistency, perseverance, and loyalty are habits that should be automatic for a Christian, and joining together as God's family to worship and give praise to Him is a result. Knowing the soon return of a triumphant Christ, the truly committed Christian should not have to think twice about attending his chosen church!

An Example of Faithfulness

When our daughter, Chrissie, was in college, she began to lose her hearing. We couldn't figure out why this was happening but remembered the time when she had developed mononucleosis and was very fatigued. Claudia had taken her to our local physician, and while they were standing at the counter checking in to the doctor's office, all of a sudden Chrissie just passed out, fell backward, and hit her head on the floor before Claudia even realized what had happened. It was after that she began losing her hearing. We have always thought that had something to do with her problem.

Anyway, she finished her bachelor's degree in Mathematics Education, got married, and moved to Moultrie, Georgia, where her husband, Jon Forehand, is a successful attorney. For the first few years they were married, she taught mathematics in public high schools and did a great job. In the meantime she had three children to take care of. As the years went by, she continued to lose more of her capacity to hear. This situation resulted in her finally having to give up teaching. She just couldn't hear the questions and comments of her students well enough to continue.

However, those obstacles haven't stopped her. She has always felt that God had His hand upon her life and has constantly been involved in church work in some way. Because she no longer was teaching, she had more time at home with the children and time to study and pray about what God had in store for her in the future. Not being able to hear was not going to stop her from being faithful to God's call and will. God led her and her family to a wonderful church of hungry, caring people, and Chrissie quickly began to get involved in the Women's Ministry group and Bible Study classes.

Before long she was president of the WM in her church and was constantly initiating new Bible study classes for the ladies in the church. Her hearing has continued to deteriorate, but you would never know it. She has difficulty even hearing someone on the telephone, so e-mail has become a blessing in our family.

Not long ago on Easter Sunday we were visiting her church in Moultrie when the pastor announced that a member of the church had accomplished something outstanding. She had gone through two years of study and had received her minister's license. When he called Chrissie's name, we were shocked! She had kept that secret from us for two years. Time has taken its toll on Chrissie's physical body. She has trouble hearing very much at all. Like her mother, she now suffers from rheumatoid arthritis that is quite painful and crippling at times. Her children are growing up so fast it's hard to keep up with all their activities, but she never gives up. In spite of the obstacles, she is doing more than ever for the kingdom of God and hardly ever slows down; she is faithful to the call. We are proud of a faithful daughter! She lives the definition of Faithfulness.

A Final Word on Faithfulness

I suppose I learned the meaning of Faithfulness early in life as we struggled in a pastor's home to make ends meet. My brothers and I worked delivering papers, bagging groceries, mowing lawns, or something like that from the time we were 10 years old. We had to if we wanted to have any money to buy what few clothes we had to wear to school and church. Dad just didn't have the extra funds to support three growing boys! Today I appreciate that kind of early training and discipline which taught me responsibility and faithfulness. As I finished high school and began my college education, I was amazed at the lack of discipline some of my fellow students displayed. I developed my study and reading habits as I progressed through school, so faithfully attending classes and completing assignments was not a problem. Of course, I was teased by my classmates about going to my room in the dorm so early and studying during the times between classes. I don't regret those habits at all, for God enabled me to stick to my goals and accomplish much during the time I served as president of Emmanuel College. Find Faithfulness first, and other fruitful habits will result!

Again, our definition of Faithfulness is "the determination to submit constantly and unfailingly my future to God through obedient loyalty, sincerity, and responsibility." Paul's words to the Corinthian Christians were, *Be on your guard, stand firm in the faith, live like men, be strong! Let everything you do be done in love* (I Cor. 16:13, Phillips). That's good advice. Proverbs 20:6 states, *Most men will proclaim every one his own goodness: but a faithful man who can find?* (KJV) That's a good question to ponder too.

Remember the parable in Matthew 25 Jesus gave about the servants and the talents? It involved the employer entrusting his servants with five talents, two talents, and one talent, respectively. His instructions were for them to use their gifts wisely according to their unique abilities. The servant with five doubled his; the servant with two did also, but the servant with one went and hid his for fear of losing it. When the lord of the servants returned, he asked how they had used these talents. Upon hearing the 100% increase by the one with five and the one with two, his words were, *Well done, thou good and faithful servant: thou hast been faithful over a few things, I will make thee ruler over many things: enter thou into the joy of thy lord* (Matt. 25:21, 23; KJV). However, he rebuked the servant with one talent who did nothing with it and gave his talent to the one with five. Then his instructions were to have the unproductive, unfaithful servant cast into outer darkness where there is weeping and gnashing of teeth (vs. 26-30).

In other words, the Fruit of Faithfulness is critical to one's eternal reward. There is no place in the kingdom of God for fear, laziness, and lack of productivity. At the conclusion of his first letter to the Christians at Thessalonica, Paul sums up the matter of faithfulness by reminding us, *He who calls you is utterly faithful and he will finish what he has set out to do* (I Thess. 5:24, Phillips). Hallelujah for the One who is utterly faithful! To live for Him in faithful service is the goal of a truly transformed Christian.

> *"Be faithful," I heard the Master say,*
> *Amid the turmoil, toil, and strife.*
> *"Did I not come to earth to show the way*
> *And on that cruel cross give my life?"*
>
> *"But, Lord," I replied, "the way is long,*
> *And I am tempted to give in.*
> *At times I cannot find a song,*
> *Whatever I try I cannot win."*

And then He gently speaks to me
With a still, small voice to calm my fears.
"Stop trying and you will be free;
Trust in my word through all the years.

"I will be there when all else fails;
Have faith and put your trust in me.
I am the wind to guide your sails
And lead you on to victory!"

CHAPTER TEN

Habit 8: Master Meekness Of Spirit And Life

Matthew 5:5 – *Happy are those who claim nothing, for the whole earth will belong to them* (Phillips).

MEEKNESS (GENTLENESS) – Uncommon courage and strength possible only when I have yielded my personal rights to God and have placed upon the altar of sacrifice anything that keeps me from being totally committed to and dependent upon God.

Have you ever wondered what it was like to be Andrew, Simon Peter's brother? Every day he heard, "Oh, you're Peter's brother, aren't you?" The poor guy had to constantly put up with Peter's boisterous, impetuous talking and acting before thinking about what he was doing. There was Peter always by the side of Jesus, monopolizing the Savior's time and jumping to conclusions, while Andrew simply stayed in the background never calling attention to himself. He just could not break into that inner circle of Peter, James, and John. Yet the Gospels record Andrew's involvement on a couple of key occasions. He actually recognized Jesus first and brought Peter to Him (John 1:40, 41) and was the disciple who brought the lad with five loaves and two fish to Jesus to feed the multitude (John 6:8). Then during the triumphal entry of Jesus into Jerusalem, some strangers came looking for Him. Andrew was there to lead them to the Master (John 12:21, 22). These brief passages reveal much about Andrew. He was not looking for personal glory; he didn't mind being in the background. He was willing to follow Jesus and do what he could to help others find Christ. Now there is a perfect illustration of Meekness.

A humble, meek man I admire greatly is Reverend John Swails. He is one of the foremost scholars of the Bible alive today, and at 90 years of age he is still very keen and insightful in his speaking. For years he taught Bible and religion courses at Emmanuel College and pastored the local Pentecostal Holiness Church. Over the years thousands of students have marveled at his knowledge of the Bible and his wisdom concerning scriptures. He served as a tremendous example of Christlike character and continues to demonstrate that Meekness is not timidity or lack of strength. While he has never aspired to be anything other than a servant of God, he possesses a nobility and dignity that draws people to him. Like Andrew, Peter's brother, John Swails has been content just to be a vessel through which the Holy Spirit can move and a spokesman for Jesus Christ. And in the last few years, while his beautiful wife, Glenda, has been in failing health and suffers from dementia, John Swails has been right by her side to take care of her. He even takes her with him on speaking trips and ministers lovingly to her needs. He knows who he is and what God has called him to be. He has always been totally committed to his God, his wife, and his family. That is enough; that is Meekness.

In our competitive, multicultured, self-centered society, Meekness is probably one of the least appreciated Fruit of the Spirit. Too often it is seen as weakness or unwillingness to compete or confront. Nothing could be further from a description of this quality of a truly transformed Christian, for Meekness is essential in emulating Christ to a confused, beleaguered world where angry people are daily slipping away from a life of fruitful purpose. Meekness in our actions and interrelationships is one of the most visible of the Fruit of the Spirit and speaks loudly to many whose lives are far from content. As always, Meekness, Love, Joy, Peace, Patience, and the other Fruit of the Spirit work together supernaturally in our daily behavior to demonstrate Christ's qualities of divine approval. And, yes, Meekness is possible to obtain as we follow the guidance of the Holy Spirit and determine to be like Jesus.

The Psalmist David said, *The meek will he guide in judgment: and the meek will he teach his way* (Psalm 25:9, KJV), and *The meek shall inherit the earth; and shall delight themselves in the abundance of peace*

(Psalm 37:11, KJV). Isaiah prophesied concerning the saints who would be rejoicing after Christ sets up His kingdom on earth, *The meek also shall increase their joy in the Lord, and the poor among men shall rejoice in the Holy One of Israel* (Isaiah 29:19, KJV). Of course, Jesus lists Meekness as one of the Beatitudes (the attitudes that ought to be) as He taught the people of Israel concepts and ideas they had never before witnessed. In the Sermon on the Mount He enumerated those aspects of attitude a truly transformed Christian ought to display. *Blessed are the meek: for they shall inherit the earth* (Matthew 5:5, KJV). J. B. Phillips translates this verse as *Happy are those who claim nothing, for the whole earth will belong to them*, and in his *Message*, paraphrasing Eugene Peterson says, *You're blessed when you're content with just who you are—no more, no less. That's the moment you find yourself proud owners of everything that can't be bought.*

Definition of Meekness
Now with that thought in mind let's look at our definition. **Meekness is uncommon courage and strength possible only when I have yielded my personal rights to God and have placed upon the altar of sacrifice anything that keeps me from being totally committed to and dependent upon God.**

    1.   First, Meekness is **uncommon**. The kind of self-sacrificing valor demonstrated by a meek person is extraordinary in today's world. The character of Jesus illustrated this uncommon action. In Matthew 11:28-30 He beautifully describes Himself like this: *Come unto me, all ye that labour and are heavy laden, and I will give you rest. Take my yoke upon you, and learn of me; for I am meek and lowly in heart: and ye shall find rest for your souls. For my yoke is easy, and my burden is light* (KJV). This kind of supernatural character is possible only through the power and inspiration of the Holy Spirit. The habit of Meekness is uncommon indeed.

    2.   Then Meekness is uncommon **courage and strength**. These two nouns signify the essence of Meekness. Other words to describe a meek temperament are *gentleness, humility, tolerance, consideration*, and *sensitivity*. The Greek word here is *prautes,* implying "an inwrought grace of the soul. We accept God's dealings with us as good and therefore without resisting."[1] As is true in many translations, there is no exact English word that corresponds to the

Greek, but Mark A. Copeland lists several aspects of translating *prautes*: "(1) To describe persons or things which have in them a certain soothing quality [e.g., having a humble and kind demeanor which calms another's anger], (2) To describe gentleness of conduct, especially on the part of people who had it in their power to act otherwise, (3) To describe the ability to take unkind remarks with good nature, (4) Most often, to describe the character in which strength and gentleness are perfectly combined."[2] Bill Gothard's definition of humility is "recognizing that God and others are actually responsible for any accomplishments in my life."[3] Similarly, his description of sensitivity is "exercising my senses so that I can perceive the true spirit and emotions of those around me."[4] Furthermore, the Greek word *prautes* is often used to refer to wild animals that have been tamed or broken. The implication here is that Meekness is not weakness. The tamed horse is still just as powerful and strong; this power is simply channeled and made productive. Courage and divine strength are embodied in the meek person's life as God channels his or her habits. Isn't it a shame to see potential wasted in a talented person's life because that person's intellect, enthusiasm, or even physical strength is undisciplined or unchanneled by the Holy Spirit's direction? Sadly, having worked with college students for many years, too often I have seen this lack of Meekness illustrated in the lives of very bright, capable young men and women. The potential was there, but it never materialized because of the lack of uncommon courage and strength made possible only through the power of the Holy Spirit. Equally, there is no place in the meek person's life for indifference, apathy, false modesty, or self-deprecation.

Robert Longman, Jr. says about gentleness, "The gift of 'gentleness' isn't about being wishy-washy, indecisive, unassertive, or just plain wimpy. It is connected instead to a refusal to use power over anyone, an unwillingness to cut and slash at people. It's about being out to build people up instead of harming them or scaring them. There are gentle ways to be bold, non-violent ways to stand up for what is right, non-manipulative ways to lead and to convince. ... If we are to be truly gentle, we need God to give us the ability to be gentle when it counts."[5]

One of the unsung heroes of American military history is General George C. Marshall. Most Americans don't remember him at all when discussions of the important Allied leaders of World War II are given. We naturally talk about Dwight D. Eisenhower, Douglas MacArthur, Winston Churchill, and Franklin D. Roosevelt, but one of the greatest and meekest leaders was George C. Marshall. He was the mastermind behind the transformation of the fledgling U.S. Army after the Japanese bombed Pearl Harbor and orchestrated the European invasion that proved to be the decisive strategy that won the war. Yet he never sought attention or the recognition for his brilliant decision-making or sensitivity to the real issues of the war. He actually mentored Eisenhower, Patton, Bradley, and other generals of the Army prior to and during World War II and was the first career soldier ever to win the Nobel Peace Prize. Later, as Secretary of State, he introduced the plan that would literally save Europe from post-war economic calamity (The Marshall Plan). He could have chosen to lead the Allied forces into Europe but instead chose Dwight D. Eisenhower to do so and remained in Washington to assist the President.[6] Now that is Meekness.

3. This uncommon courage is **possible only as I have yielded my personal rights to God**. Again, Gothard's definition of Meekness is "yielding my personal rights and expectations to God."[7] This unselfish act of submission is the key to a Christian's victorious walk with the Lord and is essential to developing habits of holiness. A part of the supernatural work of the Holy Spirit at the time of conversion is the reality that I am now a child of God ushered into His kingdom. That means that He is my King, and I am subject to His spiritual laws as well as my responsibility to the laws of my country and state. Actually, my abiding by these spiritual laws of the kingdom of God is more critical to my well being than obeying the laws of man. If I have developed the holy habits made possible through empowerment of the Fruit of the Spirit, I will have no problem obeying man's laws, but even more significant is the fact that I belong to the King of kings and Lord of lords. If anything happens to me or anyone offends me, they can take it up with Him! My life is in His hands, and I have become one of His trusted servants (as well as a brother to Jesus Christ). It's not about me or my rights

anymore. He is my defender and shield. As my loving, omnipotent, omniscient King, He is not going to let anything happen to me. He made this world and all that is in it; everything belongs to Him. I disclaim ownership of selfish possessions and material things. They are my King's; He lets me have these things so that I may bless others and develop healthy, holy habits of giving and reaching out as Jesus did.

This revelation of disclaiming ownership and yielding my rights changed my life. There is glorious freedom from bondage and guilt when Meekness is working in my life. What a blessing it is to know that I don't have to strive to accumulate earthly possessions or become independently wealthy! The realization that one doesn't really have anything anyway apart from the grace of God changes one's total purpose and perspective. Many people spend their entire lives and all their energy trying to accumulate material goods, but as the wise and wealthy King Solomon discovered at the end of his life, this attitude is nothing but vanity and emptiness. Didn't Jesus promise to take care of His own? He is totally aware of everything about me; He even knows the number of hairs in my head! We put our confidence and trust in officers of the law and elected officials of our land, but how much more God cares for His own and will protect them in all situations. No wonder Jesus said the meek would inherit the earth.

Paul eloquently describes the meek and lowly Jesus in Philippians 2:5-11: *Let Christ himself be your example as to what your attitude should be. For he, who had always been God by nature, did not cling to his prerogatives as God's equal, but stripped himself of all privilege by consenting to be a slave by nature and being born as mortal man. And, having become man, he humbled himself by living a life of utter obedience, even to the extent of dying, and the death he died was the death of a common criminal. That is why God has now lifted him so high, and has given him the name beyond all names, so that at the name of Jesus "every knee shall bow," whether in Heaven or earth or under the earth. And that is why, in the end, "every tongue shall confess" that Jesus Christ is the Lord, to the glory of God the Father* (Phillips). Sooner or later every human being who ever lived is going to have to proclaim Jesus as Lord and yield his or her rights to the King of kings. Why not do it now and be free!

4. Next, Meekness means I **have placed upon the altar of sacrifice anything that keeps me from being totally committed to and dependent upon God.** When I have yielded my rights to Him, I recognize that nothing in this world is worth losing my relationship with Christ. He becomes first and foremost in every decision I make and every step I take. Anything that hinders my walk with Christ must go—self-will, possessions, health, intellect, friends, music, schedule, activities, clothes, houses, cars, even family and friends. Did not Peter say, *Humble yourselves therefore under the mighty hand of God, that he may exalt you in due time: Casting all your care upon him; for he careth for you* (I Peter 2:6-7, KJV)? And didn't Jesus Himself say, *If any man will come after me, let him deny himself, and take up his cross, and follow me. For whosoever will save his life shall lose it: and whosoever shall lose his life for my sake shall find it* (Matthew 16:24-25, KJV)? J. B. Phillips puts verse 24 this way: *If anyone wants to follow in my footsteps he must give up all right to himself, take up his cross and follow me.* Meekness, then, implies total commitment to God. Nothing less will suffice.

Also, Meekness is being totally dependent upon God. The meek Christian realizes that he is strong, but his strength is not his own. Paul admonishes the Ephesian Christians, *Be strong in the Lord, and in the power of his might* (Ephesians 6:10, KJV). In his discussion of gentleness Father Thomas Keating states, "We labor in the service of God more than ever, and yet have the sense of stepping back and watching God make things happen according to his will both in ourselves and others. Our anxious efforts to serve God and our anguished search for God cease. Like God we labor and are at rest at the same time. We work hard but we know by experience, even bitter experience, that our efforts are not going to go anywhere except insofar as God makes them fruitful. Hence vanity, jealousy, and contention—which often accompany even our spiritual endeavors—are gradually evacuated, leaving immense freedom just to be who we are and to serve the special needs of those around us."[8] Now that is true Meekness.

The Opposite of Meekness

Surprisingly enough, the opposite of Meekness is not timidity or apathy. While these traits are certainly contrary to true Meekness, in reality the opposite of Meekness is anger. When Meekness is not operating in a person's life, human nature creates a spirit of self-absorption, a self-seeking attitude, and self-centeredness. Just as Goodness, as an attribute of God, is akin to holiness, so is Meekness. Carnality in man creates anger, which develops from a life of self-indulgence, pride, and self-righteousness.

Eventually this kind of anger will destroy a person apart from the saving power of God. Apparently even those closest to Jesus were guilty of this kind of thinking. Just before Jesus made His last entry into Jerusalem, the disciples were more concerned about who was going to be seated closest to Him on His left and right than about His crucifixion (Mark 10:35). Luke also notes that there was much discussion about who was to be the greatest in Christ's kingdom. That's when Jesus took a little child, positioned him by His side, and said, *Whosoever shall receive this child in my name receiveth me: and whosoever shall receive me receiveth him that sent me: for he that is least among you all, the same shall be great* (Luke 9:46-48, KJV). Wasn't Jesus the Master of illustration and simplicity? He quickly defined Meekness.

A Final Word on Meekness

Now we have defined Meekness as "uncommon courage and strength possible only when I have yielded my personal rights to God and have placed upon the altar of sacrifice anything that keeps me from being totally committed to and dependent upon God." Obviously, Meekness involves our interrelationships and daily actions. As we have pointed out with all the characteristics that make up the Fruit of the Spirit, Meekness becomes habitual when we are in tune with God's power and purpose for our lives. We may boast about being spiritual and say, "Thank God I am humble and meek," but until our lives actually demonstrate this kind of behavior, it's nothing but a clanking cacophony of meaningless noise.

With regard to the proper behavior related to one who has erred in the faith, Paul writes, *Brethren, if a man be overtaken in a fault, ye which are spiritual, restore such an one in the spirit of meekness; considering thyself, lest thou also be tempted* (Galatians 6:1). Again, to Timothy he instructs, *And the Lord's servant must not be a man of strife: he must be kind to all, ready and able to teach: he must have patience and the ability gently to correct those who oppose his message. He must always bear in mind the possibility that God will give them a different outlook, and that they may come to know the truth. They may come to their senses and be rescued from the power of the devil by the servant of the Lord and set to work for God's purposes* (II Timothy 2:24-26, Phillips).

I suspect that the Church of the Lord Jesus Christ would be much further along in winning the world to Him if Meekness were really practiced in our relationships.

A Meek Example

Amazingly, on a lonely night in September of 1898 a traveling salesman named John Nicholson arrived in Boscobel, Wisconsin, about 9:00 p.m. looking for a hotel room. He stopped at the Central Hotel and inquired about a room, but all the rooms were taken. The clerk said, "If you'd like, you may ask a man named Samuel Hill if you could stay in the room with him." Tired and ready for whatever rest he could find, Nicholson took the offer and prepared to retire for the night. He didn't know Samuel Hill, but at the age of 19 he had promised his dying mother that he would read the Bible every night.

Meanwhile, Mr. Hill had awakened, so Nicholson asked Hill if he would mind if he kept the light on a little longer to read and pray. Samuel Hill immediately jumped up and said, "Read it aloud. I'm a Christian too." After reading John 15, the two men knelt and prayed before sleeping. Both began to feel the need for some type of organization to assist traveling Christians like themselves. Sometime later they met again and formed an association. They decided to call it "The Gideons" after the man in the Old Testament who obeyed God and led the people of Israel to victory. Soon the idea of placing Bibles in hotel rooms across the country came up, and today over 750 million copies of Scripture have been distributed in over 70 nations.[9] Through the Gideons organization, laymen all over the world are demonstrating Meekness in proclaiming the Gospel and winning souls to Christ.

> *Amid the power struggle, O Lord, teach me to be meek*
> *And resist the urge to have my selfish way.*
> *I cannot help but want my rights and always seek*
> *Control of every day.*

Then I remember the One who came
To be a humble, sacrificial Lamb.
Upon Himself He took my shame
And forgave the sins of every man.

Savior, may I heed your voice
Speaking above the deafening roar of strife.
May I daily make your will my choice
And choose meekness as a way of life.

CHAPTER ELEVEN

Habit 9: Make Self-Control Your Goal

1 Corinthians 9:24-27 – *You've all been to the stadium and seen the athletes race. Everyone runs; one wins. Run to win. All good athletes train hard. They do it for a gold medal that tarnishes and fades. You're after one that's gold eternally. I don't know about you, but I'm running hard for the finish line. I'm giving it everything I've got. No sloppy living for me! I'm staying alert and in top condition. I'm not going to get caught napping, telling everyone else all about it and then missing out myself* (Message).

SELF-CONTROL (TEMPERANCE) – The divinely produced inward strength and discipline of my physical, mental, and spiritual being to set well-defined goals in life that lead to obeying and pleasing God.

Boy, do I wish I could play golf like Tiger Woods or Phil Mickelson! They make the game seem so easy. Hitting out of the sand or from the woods doesn't seem to bother their game at all. Those guys are good. In fact, I wish I could just beat Earl Beatty at least once. Like life, winning at golf or any sport takes dedication, endurance, determination, practice, and physical and mental ability to make it to the top. I am told that Tiger Woods spends eight hours a day hitting balls and/or lifting weights to keep in shape. Of course, part of the motivation is the million-dollar prize for the lowest score! That certainly helps.

Then we watched the winter Olympic games from Italy and were amazed at the commitment and skills of the many athletes from all over the world. The gold medal was the prize, but many of the participants knew from the beginning they didn't really have a chance for the gold. They just wanted to compete and represent their countries as best they could. In fact, many trained in a highly regimented schedule for four years without a break. Now that's self-control.

Recently on television there was a remake of the movie *The Ten Commandments*. With all the contrived dramatic license the producers took, I still thought the character of Moses was quite believable. He demonstrated the Fruit of the Spirit in his dealings with Pharaoh and the people of Israel. Man, did he have to have self-control. Those Israelites were never satisfied. God performed miracle after miracle on their behalf, yet Moses had to listen to their murmuring and complaining for forty years. Day after day someone kept plotting to deceive him or usurp his authority, but he continued to wait upon God's orders and direction. Now Moses wasn't perfect; he did get aggravated and struck the rock the second time rather than just speak to it as God directed. Nevertheless, he had to exhibit exemplary self-control through all that ordeal of the desert wanderings.

Definition of Self-Control

Now our definition of Self-Control is this: **The divinely produced inward strength and discipline of my physical, mental, and spiritual being to set well-defined goals in life that lead to obeying and pleasing God.**

1. First, Self-Control must be **divinely produced**. We use the term "self-control," but there really must be "Spirit-Control" at work. Man cannot within himself ever hope to control his own decision-making and ability to exercise spiritual discipline. As with all the Fruit, each is of the Spirit, not man-made. Self-Control is a product of the indwelling of the Holy Spirit, a transformation of character possible only by faith and yielding my life to Christ. Believing that Jesus shed his blood, died on the cross, and rose from the dead restores the glory of God, and intimacy with Him not possible without the Holy Spirit's supernatural power. When my life is Spirit-controlled, the Holy Spirit is freely flowing into and filling every part of my being. Bill Gothard gives an interesting definition for Self-Control: "Instant obedience to the initial promptings of God's Spirit."[1] And immediately following his listing of the Fruit of the Spirit, the

Apostle Paul states, *And they that are Christ's have crucified the flesh with the affections and lusts. If we live in the Spirit, let us also walk in the Spirit* (Galatians 5:24-25, KJV). What Paul is saying is that man's carnal nature restricts him from having the ability to exercise restraint and control over his life. That is where the habits of Goodness, Faithfulness, and Meekness operate simultaneously with Self-Control. Only the Holy Spirit can prompt a person and prevent him from giving in to his carnal nature to sin.

2.   Then Self-Control is **the inward strength and discipline** that are divinely produced. The Greek word here is *egkrateia*, meaning "one holding himself in."[2] No person can find the necessary inward strength and discipline to cope with life without exercising Self-Control. This Fruit made possible by the Holy Spirit is essential to avoid yielding to temptation. Paul compares the self-control of a Christian to that of a runner in a race. In I Corinthians 9:25-27 he describes this event: *Every competitor in athletic events goes into serious training. Athletes will take tremendous pains—for a fading crown of leaves. But our contest is for an eternal crown that will never fade. I run the race then with determination. I am no shadowboxer; I really fight! I am my body's sternest master, for fear that when I have preached to others I should myself be disqualified* (Phillips). Paul was obviously a fighter. A normal person would never have survived all he endured, but he knew Self-Control. You can hear the determination in his voice as he writes, *This priceless treasure we hold, so to speak, in a common earthenware jar—to show that the splendid power of it belongs to God and not to us. We are handicapped on all sides, but we are never frustrated; we are puzzled, but never in despair. We are persecuted, but we never have to stand it alone: we may be knocked down but we are never knocked out* (II Cor. 4:7-9, Phillips).

He goes on to say, *The first time I had to defend myself no one was on my side—they all deserted me, God forgive them! Yet the Lord himself stood by me and gave me strength to proclaim the message clearly and fully, so that the Gentiles could hear it, and I was rescued "from the lion's mouth." I am sure the Lord will rescue me from every evil plot, and will keep me safe until I reach his heavenly kingdom* (II Timothy 4:16-18, Phillips); and in the same letter, *As for me, I feel that the last drops of my life are being poured out for God. The glorious fight that God gave me I have fought, the course that I was set I have finished, and I have kept the faith. The future for me holds the crown of righteousness which God, the true judge, will give me in that day—and not, of course, only to me but to all those who have loved what they have seen of him* (II Timothy 4:6-8, Phillips). You can't do it by yourself.

3.   Then Self-Control is the discipline **of my physical**, **mental**, **and spiritual being**. Paul reminds us in I Corinthians 6:19-20, *What? Know ye not that your body is the temple of the Holy Ghost which is in you, which ye have of God, and ye are not your own? For ye are bought with a price: therefore glorify God in your body, and in your spirit, which are God's* (KJV). Human willpower is not adequate when it comes to resisting the myriad temptations and trials we face every day. Until a person has totally yielded his rights and his being to God, he will not be able to cope with the stress of this life. Many people in our self-indulgent, undisciplined society have allowed the cravings of their bodies to overcome their spiritual man and their souls (mind, will, and emotions). Every day we read in the newspapers or hear on TV or radio news about those who have done harm to themselves and others because of drunkenness, drug use, adultery, fornication, robbery, or rioting, all results of a lack of divinely inspired Self-Control. Even the nasty habit of smoking proves that we cannot stop indulging by ourselves, and attempts by the government or social agencies to scare individuals into quitting don't work. Actually, America is also a nation plagued with obesity largely because we have too much food and cannot control our eating habits. Even aspects of our lives that are not considered sinful indulgences may become hindrances to our spiritual well-being when we cannot control our urges.

Much of the problem resides in the space between our ears. Self-Control includes a renewed mind. The transformation that takes place when we come to Christ includes our entire being, and a very important part of who we are is the brain. Holy habits such as developing Love, Joy, Peace, Patience, and the other Fruit of the Spirit include the changes that supernaturally occur in our behavior as we discipline the mind, submit the will, and control the emotions.

I remember when our children were young, we endeavored to instill into their hearts and minds key scriptures. Every morning before Mark and Chrissie went to school, we would recite particular verses and discuss their meaning. A difficult section for us to memorize was II Corinthians 10:3-5, but through the years we have lived by those verses: *For though we walk in the flesh, we do not war after the flesh: (For the weapons of our warfare are not carnal, but mighty through God to the pulling down of strong holds;) Casting down imaginations, and every high thing that exalteth itself against the knowledge of God, and bringing into captivity every thought to the obedience of Christ* (KJV). *The Message* paraphrases those verses this way: *The world is unprincipled. It's dog-eat-dog out there! The world doesn't fight fair. But we don't live or fight our battles that way—never have and never will. The tools of our trade aren't for marketing or manipulation, but they are for demolishing that entire, massively corrupt culture. We use our powerful God-tools for smashing warped philosophies, tearing down barriers erected against the truth of God, fitting every loose thought and emotion and impulse into the structure of life shaped by Christ. Our tools are ready at hand for clearing the ground of every obstruction and building lives of obedience into maturity.* What a great description of the habits of holiness that are created in us when we become like Christ! The Fruit of the Spirit are the "God-tools" Eugene Peterson is talking about in this passage. As a person learns to control his mind, will, and emotions by submitting to the Holy Spirit and allowing God to clear his life of every carnal obstruction, he becomes a powerful warrior in the army of the Lord.

4.   Further, Self-Control involves the inward strength **to set well-defined goals in life**. Unless a person sees the complete picture, prays, and plans for the future, he will not be able to fulfill God's purpose for his life. Paul's illustration of competing in a race is fitting at this point. Spirit-filled Christians have a sure goal in focus and are determined to do whatever is necessary to reach the prize. As we focus upon the results of our earthly journey, we subordinate everything else to the will and purpose of following Christ. The presence of the Holy Spirit in our lives and the operation of the Fruit of the Spirit through holy habits every step of the way inspire us to

follow Jesus. It is important to set well-defined goals, a pattern of behavior that will make each goal possible, and a determined route to complete that goal. Concentrating upon well-written, intelligent spiritual goals, including the conscious application of the Fruit of the Spirit, will keep a focus on the essentials and bring maturity to the life of a truly transformed Christian. Let the Holy Spirit do the rest. Rick Warren points out, "Living the rest of your life for the glory of God will require a change in your priorities, your schedule, your relationships, and everything else. It will sometimes mean choosing a difficult path instead of an easy one. Even Jesus struggled with this. … You face the same choice. Will you live for your own goals, comfort, and pleasure, or will you live the rest of your life for God's glory, knowing that he has promised eternal rewards?"[3]

5.   Finally, to achieve Self-Control in his life a truly transformed Christian needs to establish well-defined goals **that lead to obeying and pleasing God**. Knowing the limitations of this earthly existence and keeping his eye on the eternal prize will help a person set goals that focus upon obeying and pleasing God. After all, paramount among reasons for living are goals that glorify Him. Setting goals of prayer, daily devotional time, corporate worship, and family activities would certainly be appropriate and pleasing to God. In fact, the Fruit of the Spirit is not going to be developed in a life void of these goals. Healthy, holy habits result from intentional, deliberate actions that are inspired by one's walk with the Lord of a daily basis. There are no shortcuts or omissions here.

Controlling Our Speech

One of the telltale signs of a lack of Self-Control is our conversation and verbal interaction with others. In fact, in chapter 3 of his letter the very practical James writes that the secret of Self-Control is control of the tongue. Words can be lifesaving or deadly. They betray the true character of a person and reveal the innermost thoughts. Without the help of the Holy Spirit we cannot bridle the tongue or keep from bitter accusations and self-promoting barbs. One of the primary goals to set to achieve Self-Control is guarding our speech. Emily Dickinson observed, "A word is dead when it is said, some say. I say it just begins to live that day."[4] In her simple, poetic way she made a profound statement. If we only realized that our words are eternal, we would be much more careful about uttering negative, destructive comments. God's heavenly computer stores up every word we say, and one day we will have to account for our actions. Actually, if we knew all our secret thoughts and actions were to be exposed, I wonder how different our lives would be.

Obviously, Jesus is our best example of Self-Control. When Satan confronted Him with temptations in the wilderness, He repeatedly resisted the urge to give in to his physical needs or human inclinations and spoke the truth in boldness and faith. Even on the cross He exhibited uncommon courage and self-control as He died. Jesus never lost control. What a Savior!

Make "Spirit-Control" Your Goal

Once again, our definition of Self-Control or Temperance is "the divinely produced inward strength and discipline of my physical, mental, and spiritual being to set well-defined goals in life that lead to obeying and pleasing God." In a world of decadent self-indulgence, undisciplined excess, mental intemperance, and uncontrolled emotions, only divinely produced Self-Control will conquer sin. Self-reliance upon human willpower is insufficient. Self-imposed abstinence isn't the answer. Self-righteousness will fail. Human rehabilitation programs won't do the job. In reality government funding often leads to misappropriation and mismanagement of the taxpayers' money. Only "Spirit-controlled" lives will succeed.

I have always been an admirer of David Wilkerson and his Teen Challenge organization. His program takes drug addicts off the streets of our cities and first teaches them discipline and submission to Christ. Every effort is made to persuade them to become Christians first, and then God will help them to overcome these addictions. The rate of successful rehabilitation in Teen Challenge is far greater than that of any government program. That's because conversion must precede self-control. We can't be overcomers alone. True Self-Control can come only from repentance and dependence upon God's direction and goals for my life.

> *Lord, I give up and relinquish control,*
> *Allowing you to direct my way.*
> *Tame my foolish heart and tongue and guide my steps each day.*
> *I have made up my mind and will remain true,*

Regardless of the fears I face or what other people do.
Spirit-control is the key to joy, not my stubborn, selfish will.
When I determine to let you lead, you take me to that hill
Where you were always in control, and paid the price for me.
Perfect self-control led to the cross where you died on Calvary.

CHAPTER TWELVE

Remain Fruitful

John 15:16 – *Ye have not chosen me, but I have chosen you, and ordained you, that ye should go and bring forth fruit, and that your fruit should remain: that whatsoever ye shall ask of the Father in my name, he may give it to you* (KJV).

"If I Were the Devil"

I would gain control of the most powerful nation in the world.

I would delude their minds into thinking that they had come from man's efforts, instead of God's blessings.

I would promote an attitude of loving things and using people, instead of the other way around.

I would dupe entire states into relying on gambling for their state revenue.

I would convince people that character is not an issue when it comes to leadership.

I would make it legal to take the life of unborn babies.

I would make it socially acceptable to take one's own life, and invent machines to make it convenient.

I would cheapen human life as much as possible so that lives of animals are valued more than human beings.

I would take God out of the schools, where even the mention of

His name was grounds for a lawsuit.

I would come up with drugs that sedate the mind and target the young, and I would get sports heroes to advertise them.

I would get control of the media, so that every night I could pollute the minds of every family member for my agenda.

I would attack the family, the backbone of any nation; I would make divorce acceptable and easy, even fashionable. If the family crumbles, so does the nation.

I would compel people to express their most depraved fantasies on canvas and movie screens, and I would call it art.

I would convince the world that people are born homosexuals, and that their lifestyles should be accepted and marveled.

I would convince the people that right and wrong are determined by a few who call themselves authorities and refer to their agendas as politically correct.

I would persuade people that the church is irrelevant and out of date; the Bible is for the naïve.

I would dull the minds of Christians, and make them believe that prayer is not important, and that faithfulness and obedience are optional.

I GUESS I WOULD LEAVE THINGS PRETTY MUCH THE WAY THEY ARE!

Paul Harvey (1999)

Spring is an amazing time of the year. To see the earth springing forth with green grass, multicolored flowers, and vibrant foliage on trees that had been bare just a few days before is nothing short of miraculous. God reminds us every spring that He is still there and that the resurrection is a reality. Likewise, apple, peach, cherry, and orange trees that have been living for many years once again come alive with blossoms that will turn into delicious, nourishing fruit. Blueberry, blackberry, and grape vines also join in the celebration of God's grandeur as they yield such tantalizing fruit. When life is present, fruit continues!

In the 17th century there lived in France a quiet man who came to be known as Brother Lawrence. He is remembered primarily because of his devout Christian life and his letters that were published after his death. In his testimony he recalled, "God did me a glorious favor in bringing me to a conversion at the age of eighteen. In the winter I saw a tree stripped of its leaves and I knew that within a little time the leaves would be renewed, and that afterwards the flowers and the fruit would appear. From this I received a high view of the power and providence of God which has never since departed from my soul. The view I grasped that day set me completely loose from the world and kindled in me such a love for God that I cannot tell whether it has increased during the more than forty years since that time."[1]

Bearing fruit is essential for a Christian. Continued fruit-bearing is required if Christ is to be exalted. Jesus made it so simple and clear. Listen to his words in John 15: *I am the real vine; my Father is the vinedresser. He removes any of my branches which are not bearing fruit and he prunes every branch that does bear fruit to increase its yield. Now you have already been pruned by my words. You must go on growing in me and I will grow in you. For just as the branch cannot bear any fruit unless it shares the life of the vine, so you can produce nothing unless you go on growing in me. I am the vine itself; you are the branches. It is the man who shares my life and whose life I share who proves faithful. For the plain fact is that apart from me you can do nothing at all. The man who does not share my life is like a branch that is broken off and withers away. He becomes just like the dry sticks that men pick up and use for firewood. But if you live your life in me, and my words live in your hearts, you can ask for whatever you like and it will come true for you. This is how my Father will be glorified—in your becoming fruitful and being my disciples* (Phillips).

There you have it. These words contain the formula for success for a truly transformed Christian. As always, Jesus is the answer and has the answer. His message is always the same; share his life and you will continue to produce fruit, more fruit, and much fruit. Apart from him you are nothing and can do nothing. This is a lesson that is so difficult for us humans to understand, yet He explained it specifically. For the truly transformed Christian, life consists of being connected to the Vine. As the life-giving power of the Holy Spirit flows through our beings because we are inseparably attached to Christ, we grow continuously and can produce the Fruit of the Spirit in increasingly mature ways. Read the above passage in John 15 again. Check it out in other translations. These are the words of Jesus, our risen Lord! Let the truth and depth of this simple description sink into your spirit.

Read it again! See how the maturation process is sometimes painful. God the Father, the Almighty Vinedresser, is constantly pruning productive branches in order for them to increase production. In Georgia and South Carolina there are many peach orchards. Every fall the caretaker of the orchard cuts off the dead branches and prunes the trees so that their yield in the coming year will be an abundant crop of ripe, delicious fruit. I have seen piles and piles of branches removed from the small, unattractive peach trees, but the next spring they grow more live branches than ever that bear large, luscious peaches. We are like those branches. Jesus said that His words are part of the pruning process, and if we are to follow Him, we heed those divine instructions. The Fruit of the Spirit is produced simply by growing in Him as He lives in us. Life's trials and setbacks must be seen as times of pruning and preparing for greater future growth as children of the King. The way for us to bear more fruit and much fruit is to continue to allow the Vinedresser to take away anything that is deadly—our self-dependency, our selfish ambition, our defiant attitudes, our self-righteousness, our accumulation of wealth—anything keeping us from following Him with all our hearts. Pruning is essential for fruit-bearing.

Efficiency or Effectiveness?

Let me explain it another way. Some time ago I heard Dr. Doug Beacham, executive director of World Missions for the International Pentecostal Holiness Church, speak on a Sunday morning in our local church. His insights upon John 15:16 were inspiring and illuminating. He basically shared his heart concerning a life that is productive for the kingdom of God. His mention of Peter Drucker brought to my memory the writings of this management guru whose teachings have literally revolutionized the world of industry and business. Drucker clarified many aspects of operating a successful business or organization. One of his well-known statements is, "There is nothing so useless as doing efficiently that which should not be done at all."[2] His definition of *efficiency* is "doing things right." However, more important is *effectiveness*, "doing the right things right." To quote him exactly, "Management is doing things right. Leadership is doing the right things."[3] In other words, it's not how many hours you put in that matters; it's what you do during those hours that counts. A person may be extremely efficient at what he does, but what he does might be wasting time and unproductive if he isn't concentrating upon the right objectives. The fruit-producing life is effective!

Here is an important lesson for a truly transformed Christian. For many years I served as president of a Christian college. During that time I constantly had to make decisions about the best plan of action and the most productive ways to create the best possible environment for learning for college students. The students who chose Emmanuel College were looking for a different kind of experience from what they would receive at a secular, publicly operated college or university. Sometimes I fell into the trap of trying to please or impress men with my uncanny ability to make decisions or raise money, but I always came back to the real reasons I was in the position I had—to please God and build a school where students could find answers to their many questions about living in a sinful, corrupt, anti-Christian world. I discovered that my worth to God as an individual did not depend upon how successful I was at raising money or influencing donors. My value to the kingdom was more than a job description or set of criteria created by man. Who I am is what God made me uniquely to be. To produce the Fruit of the Spirit is the ultimate reason for living. All else is secondary to that purpose. Regardless of his or her profession or secular job, a truly transformed Christian keeps a clear perspective. Following Jesus and emulating His character are eternal goals. The effective Christian life is growing in the Fruit of the Spirit and allowing those holy habits to become a part of my daily interaction with my family, friends, fellow employees, church congregation, and even strangers.

Remember the Root Command

Read on in that 15th chapter of John. Jesus continues, *I've told you these things for a purpose: that my joy might be your joy, and your joy fully mature. This is my command: Love one another the way I loved you. This is the best way to love. Put your life on the line for your friends. You are my friends when you do the things I command you. I'm no longer calling you servants because servants don't understand what their master is thinking and planning. No, I've named you friends because I've let you in on everything I've heard from the Father. You didn't choose me, remember; I chose you, and put you in the world to bear fruit, fruit that won't spoil. As fruit bearers, whatever you ask the Father in relation to me, he gives you. But remember the root command: Love one another* (John 15:11-17, Msg).

Holy habits are everyday occurrences for the truly transformed Christian. As we grow and are nurtured by the True Vine, we learn the secret of effective, successful living. This intimate, organic connection to Christ is achieved through focusing daily upon His Word and the Holy Spirit's guidance. Fruit will come. Growth and maturity will occur. Verse 17 above, in the paraphrasing of Eugene Peterson, identifies the "root command" – Love. Knowing Christ and putting into practice His teachings and example is the only way to live. Living the root command means letting Love be your guide at all times. The lifeline of the connection to the root provides the nourishment, flow of the Spirit, and sustenance always needed to produce fruit.

The Secret of the Living Seed

Remember the parable Jesus used about the farmer sowing seed? *There was once a man who went out to sow. In his sowing some of the seeds fell by the roadside and the birds swooped down and gobbled them up. Some fell on stony patches where they had very little soil. They sprang up quickly in the shallow soil, but when the sun came up they were scorched by the heat and withered away because they had no roots. Some seeds fell among thorn bushes, and the thorns grew up and choked the life out of them. But some fell on good soil and produced a crop—thirty times* (Matthew 13:3-8, Phillips). In this parable is the key to bearing Fruit. Jesus went on to explain his meaning: *Now listen to the parable of the sower. When a man hears the message of the kingdom and does not grasp it, the evil one comes and snatches away what was sown in his heart. This is like the seed sown by the wayside. The seed sown on the stony patches represents the man who hears the message and eagerly accepts it. But it has not taken root in him and does not last long—the moment trouble or persecution arises through the message he gives up his faith at once. The seed sown among the thorns represents the man who hears the message, and then the worries of this life and the illusions of wealth choke it to death and so it produces no "crop" in his life. But the seed sown on good soil is the man who both hears and understands the message. His life shows a good crop, a hundred, sixty or thirty times what was sown* (Matthew 3:18-23, Phillips). Continually and increasingly bearing Fruit, then, is essential as we cling to the True Vine and become rooted and grounded in the Word of God. The secret of productive fruit-bearing and spiritual growth is in our connection to the source of life and acting upon the words and life of Jesus, our Lord.

So we conclude our study of the Fruit of the Spirit by coming full circle back to our chapter on Love. Fruit remains and feeds others when we love as Jesus loved. When we love God and others as Jesus did, joy is full, peace is abundant, patience persists, kindness is kindled, goodness is illuminated, faithfulness is found, meekness abounds, and self-control is accomplished. Then and only then will a Christian make a difference in this world. Until a person has established a lifestyle of decision-making and behavior based upon the operation of the Fruit of the Spirit in his life, he will have missed the greatest opportunity to produce a life of abundant, fruitful, meaningful fulfillment of God's purpose and Christ's example. Don't miss the adventure.

The righteous shall flourish like the palm tree:
He shall grow like a cedar in Lebanon.
Those that be planted in the house of the Lord
Shall flourish in the courts of our God.
They shall still bring forth fruit in old age;
They shall be fat and flourishing;
To show that the Lord is upright:
He is my rock, and there is no unrighteousness in him.
Psalm 92:12-15, KJV

REFERENCES

Introduction

1. Bob Moorehead, "The Paradox of Our Age," *Words Aptly Spoken* (Kirkland, WA: Overlake Christian Press, 1995).

2. Charles Colson and Nancy Pearcey, *How Now Shall We Live?* (Wheaton, IL: Tyndale House Publishers, Inc., 1999), x.

3. *Ibid.*, p. x.

4. *Ibid.*, p. xii.

Chapter I

1. C. S. Lewis, *The Case for Christianity* (New York: Walker and Company, 1987), 9.

2. Richard J. Enrico, "The Devil's Convention," Foundation for Moral Restoration, Chantilly, VA (www.icwseminary.org/convention.htm).

3. Stephen Covey, *The Seven Habits of Highly Effective People* (New York: Fireside, Simon & Schuster, 1990.)

4. *Ibid.*, p. 47.

5. *Ibid.*

6. C. S. Lewis, *op. cit.,* p. 94.

Chapter II

1. C. S. Lewis, *Mere Christianity* ("C. S. Lewis Quote Page," www.comnet.net/~rex/cslewis.htm).

Chapter III

1. Steve Saint, "Interview with John W. Kennedy," *Today's Pentecostal Evangel*, April 16, 2006, p. 14.

2. Mark A. Copeland, "The Flesh and the Spirit: The Fruit of the Spirit," *Executable Outlines*, 2006 (www.ccel.org/contrib/exec_outlines/fs/fs_09.htm).

Chapter IV

1.   Billy Sunday, quoted by Mark A. Copeland in his outline on "The Fruit of the Spirit—Joy," page 2, (www.ccel.org/contrib/exec_outlines/fs/fs_10.htm).

2.   Mark J. Young, "Fruit," *Mark J. Young's Bible Study Materials* (www.mjyoung.net/bible/fruit.htm).

3.   C. S. Lewis ("C. S. Lewis Quote Page," www.comnet.net/~rex/cslewis.htm).

4.   *Ibid.*

5.   C. S. Lewis, *Surprised by Joy: The Shape of My Early Life*, "Chapter XIV," (1955). Chapter XIV quoted online under "In Their Own Words" at www.pbs.org/wgbh/questionofgod/ownwords/joy.html.

6.   W. E. Vine, *Vine's Concise Dictionary of the Bible* (Nashville,TN: Thomas Nelson, Inc., 2005), 200.

7.   "Decide for Happiness," Article quoted from www.hbingham.com/musings/happiness.htm.

Chapter V

1. Horatio G. Spafford, "It Is Well with My Soul," *Worship His Majesty* (Alexandria, IN: Gaither Music Company, 1987), 524.

Chapter VI

1.   Robert J. Morgan, *On This Day* (Nashville, TN: Thomas Nelson Publishers, 1997), March 12.

2.   *Ibid.*

3.   W. E. Vine, *op. cit.*, p. 222.

4.   *Ibid.*

5.   Bill Gothard, "Character Qualities, (www.billgothard.com/bill/teaching/characterqualities/.

6.   *Ibid.*

7.   Father Thomas Keating, *Fruits and Gifts of the Spirit* (www.centering prayer.com/fruits).

Chapter VII

1. W. E. Vine, *op. cit.*, p. 206.
2. *Ibid.*
3. Bill Gothard, *op. cit.*
4. William Shakespeare, "Act I, Scene IV," *Macbeth*, in David Daiches et. al., *English Literature* (Boston: Houghton Mifflin Co., 1968), 151.

Chapter VIII

1. C. S. Lewis, *The Case for Christianity*, *op. cit.*, p. 95.
2. W. E. Vine, *op. cit.*, p. 160.

Chapter IX

1. Bill Gothard, *op. cit.*
2. W. E. Vine, *op. cit.*, p. 129.
3. Stephen Covey, *op. cit.*, p. 95.
4. Gothard, *op. cit.*
5. *Ibid.*

Chapter X

1. W. E. Vine, *op. cit.,* p. 236.
2. Mark A. Copeland, *op. cit.*
3. Gothard, *op. cit.*
4. *Ibid.*
5. Robert Longman, Jr. (www.spirithome.com/fruitssp.html).
6. Jack Uldrich, **Soldier, Stateman, Peacemaker: Leadership Lessons from George C. Marshall** (New York: American Management Association, 2005).
7. Gothard, *op. cit.*
8. Keating, *op. cit.*
9. Robert J. Morgan, *op. cit.*, July 1.

Chapter XI

1. Gothard, *op. cit.*
2. W. E. Vine, *op. cit.*, p. 374.
3. Rick Warren, *The Purpose Driven Life* (Grand Rapids, MI: Zondervan, 2002), 57.
4. Emily Dickinson, "A Word," *Adventures for Americans* (Second Edition, Helen C. Derrick et. al., New York: Harcourt, Brace & World, Inc., 1962), 546.

Chapter XII

1. Brother Lawrence & Frank Laubach, *Practicing His Presence* (Jacksonville, FL: SeedSowers Publishing, 1973), 41.
2. Peter Drucker, "The Quotations Page" (www.quotationspage.com/quotes/Peter_Drucker/-22k).
3. *Ibid.*